GHOSTS ALONG THE ROAD

An offbeat look off the beaten path in a special
part of Rhode Island and Connecticut

by

RONA MANN

authorHOUSE

1663 Liberty Drive, Suite 200
Bloomington, Indiana 47403
(800) 839-8640
www.authorhouse.com

First published by AuthorHouse 08/12/04

ISBN: 1-4184-4624-6 (sc)

Library of Congress Control Number: 2004096220

Printed in the United States of America
Bloomington, Indiana

This book is printed on acid-free paper.

Dedication Page

To Pat Grande who had the idea...

To Janie Carlisle who pushed it into reality...

To Dave who gives me a push at the beginning of every new road, and is always there at the end, waiting for me with unfailing and unconditional love and support....

And most of all, this book is dedicated to the men and women who came so many years ago to this region with nothing more than what was on their backs, and set about to build the roads and homes and mills and a society, while never once forgetting their first obligation was to the land itself.

May their ghosts never cease to inhabit these roads, forever peaking around corners at curious travelers, urging them on to find for themselves the secrets that were uncovered so very long ago.

Contents

Foreword

"I shall be telling this with a sigh
Somewhere ages and ages hence:
Two roads diverged in a wood, and I ---
I took the one less traveled by,
And that has made all the difference"
...Robert Frost, THE ROAD NOT TAKEN

Who doesn't know this poem? Whether it was crammed down your throat in some high school American Literature class, or perhaps something you heard quoted in later life and didn't know from whence it came, the words nevertheless awaken feelings; and to me, awakening feelings in the reader is the very zenith of successful writing.

There has never been a back way, a dirt road, or an unpaved adventure I haven't been willing to take. Roads like this beckon to me, seducing me, urging me to take the first few steps, or drive a mile down their bumpy paths.

At the southwestern tip of Rhode Island the shoreline kisses the southeastern border of Connecticut and is a fascinating place to begin exploring these roads. If you're a pessimist, you'll see only the potholes. But if you're the least bit curious, just throw away the map and step where you don't know how or where the road will end. Then just put out your hand and open your eyes wide.

Let a ghost take it from there.

R.M.

The Road To Alton: 02830

If you love the history of a place even though the place isn't very large, then the spirit of wanderlust should help you point your vehicle toward that tiny part of Richmond called Alton.

Most have heard of it; few know exactly where it is. So hop in, fasten that seat belt, and head for the southwestern portion of Richmond, only a few miles up the road from Westerly.

From Dunns Corners, proceed on the Westerly Bradford Road through the village of Bradford framed on one side by the Pawcatuck River. When you get to the junction of Rt. 91 and Woodville Alton Road you've more or less arrived.

Alton isn't a thriving village as much as it is a statement of how history shapes an area and its people. There are no tourist attractions here, no shopping centers, no obvious landmarks; but if you do a little searching, you can find the pearl in the oyster known as Alton Village.

In 1757 a section of the new township of Richmond was sold to Samuel Kinyon of Charleston. This flat stretch of land contained just over 170 acres and had little more than bushes, trees, and a boundary of the Pawcatuck River.

After a history of many land transfers from one family to another, in 1860 a well known manufacturer named David Aldrich paid $350. for 36 acres of the land between the Wood and Pawcatuck Rivers so that he could build a mill village. Aldrich accomplished this goal, and the mill ran strictly by water power for years. He built a highway and even a few tenements. Aldrich called the area Plainville after the area that had previously been known as "The Plains," and his own personal property, "Plainville Mill Estate."

The mill made fine woolen cassimirs, a kind of plain or twilled woolen cloth. Not long after, Aldrich produced cheap blankets that were used in the Civil War and generated a greater profit.

After the war, Aldrich deeded a lot on which to erect a place of worship. The locals pledged their funds as there was no house of worship nearby. One of the first "contributions" was the proceeds from a strawberry festival, a tidy sum of $105.38 that was added to the coffers of the building fund. Area firms were enlisted to make donations, and even the Providence and Stonington Railroad coughed up $13.75 toward the effort. The building cost $1205.60, the local Rockville contractor earned $1000. for the church's construction, and incorporation was filed under the name Wood River Chapel Society.

In 1880 the mill property was sold to William Walton and William Blakely. Walton was from England, trained by his parents to be an expert weaver. After coming to America, he quickly rose

1

from mill operator to overseer. His next dream was to create a model village. The W was dropped from his name and thus Alton was born.

Together Walton and Blakely planted 200 maple trees in the area in addition to building new homes, laying new sidewalks, and providing each homeowner with an acre of land for a garden that was fertilized and plowed yearly at the company's expense.

Walton did not stop there however. He organized a fire company, a ball team, and a coronet band. He gave clambakes every summer with large amounts of food, music for dancing, and no speeches whatsoever! The clambakes were held in Myrtle Grove; today Myrtle Avenue just off Rt. 91 offers name recognition to those pleasures of past years.

The chapel was the center of Alton's social life. Its funding continued to thrive from the Ladies Sewing Circle, socials, fairs, suppers, and festivals, and from renting the property for lectures, shows, club meetings, and entertainment.

In 1898 during a long and particularly bad winter, fire consumed the structure, and life in the village slowed considerably. Walton decided not to rebuild due to other business dealings at the time; and many families, now without a means of income, moved away. The village store only opened for an hour or two a day, and even then, rarely turned a profit.

It was not until 1906 that Alton was reborn. Wood River Mills was sold to Jacob Curry of Boston who sold the estate, land, and buildings just two days later to the Alton Manufacturing Co. with rights and title to the river, mill pond, bridge, dam, streets, and highway. They began making delicate lace, erected two new buildings, and installed the most complicated textile looms ever made. Employment in the village thrived once again.

Less than two years later the Alton Manufacturing Co. was bankrupt and the property was once again sold. Now it was called the Richmond Lace Works, and this mill seemed to flourish until 1917 when the lace weavers went out on strike for such a long time that the mill was never the same. The mood was bleak; old relationships were severed. Many people moved away, and the company was forced to operate only part time.

In 1927 a bad flood washed out the bridges and the mill was badly damaged, yet the mill continued to produce some of the finest laces ever made in America. In 1962 due to cheaper priced European imports and changing styles, the plant was sold for a mere $120,000 to Charbert, Inc. the maker of elastic fabrics. Today Charbert is known worldwide as a major textile manufacturer. Its main plant is the one in Alton, employing 100 people. Another 65 people work at the second mill in Peacedale, according to Bonnie Jacob, Director of Human Resources.

The tiny chapel with a long history became what is now St. Thomas Episcopal Church, an active member of the Providence Diocese.

The social activities that were so prevalent at the old chapel now live on at the Alton Volunteer Fire Company which serves as the touchstone of the community's social events. If you drive by the fire company and check out the sign, there is always a dinner or social event in the offing.

So it appears on the surface that the modern day Alton doesn't have a great deal to offer... unless you take another look. While we are so used to looking at the facades of shops, restaurants, and businesses, it is only when they don't exist that it forces the traveller to look a little deeper to find the charm. And what treasures Alton has for the curious!

Jack Martin, a painting and decorating contractor who works in the area although his residence is in Wickford, sings the praises of modern-day Alton.

"It's truly the country," said Martin in a recent interview. "There's some of the best fishing in New England, beautiful woods for camping, and it seems to me that just about everybody who lives in Alton has at least one pickup truck."

Martin, who is currently working on Homestead Road, a narrow residential road off the Carolina-Alton Road (Rt. 91), fishes and canoes in Alton reguarly.

"The trout in Meadowbrook Pond are some of the best," offers Martin. "It's a ritual that the second Saturday in April is the opening of trout season, and many people come to Alton and camp out in the woods the night before. It's cold; some say Alton's the coldest place in Rhode Island, but a tradition's a tradition."

Martin also sings the praises of Alton Pond, accessible only by canoe, and known for its cypress tree stumps and large mouth bass.

"No motorized boats are allowed, only electric trawling motors or rowing or canoes."

The Wood River feeds right into Alton Pond (some call it the Wood River Pond), and the locals will tell you there is no better fishing in the state.

But then you'll have to see for yourself as you continue to travel this "road less travelled" ...this time to tiny, lovely Alton.

RONA MANN

The Road To Ashaway: 02804

It's a place we all know, but few know well.

Motorists rush through it on their way to either Westerly or Hopkinton or Rt. 95.

It is a stretch of state road to most...a means to an end.

To those who live there, however, it is steeped in rich history. It has charm, it has ghosts, it has roots and wings. It is Ashaway.

Ashaway is a village in the town of Hopkinton comprised of approximately 578 families or 1584 people. Small, even by Rhode Island standards.

It's not hard to see why people aren't quite sure if it's a part of Westerly, or is, in fact, part of Hopkinton City, as it has a land area of only about 5 miles. But oh, what Ashaway does with those 5 miles!

Although many people are familiar with Ashaway strictly from Main Street (Rt. 3), the profile and charm of the village lies in what you find when you get off the beaten path.

It is difficult to recommend which road you should turn down, because each road taken yields something else . Sprawling farms, large, stately homes rich in history, and a world famous factory that everyone knows of, but few people know about.

So perhaps we should start here at Ashaway Line and Twine, founded in 1824 by Capt. Lester Crandall, and still operated today by the sixth generation of the Crandall family.

The little factory that occupies that pale green building on High St. (Rt. 216) is a world leader in the production of surgical suture thread and custom braided products for the textile industry, for fly fishing lines, and for many other applications. But Ashaway Line and Twine is best known as the only U.S. manufacturer of racket strings for tennis, squash, racquetball, and badminton.

Just around the corner from the factory is West Street, a curious and unassuming street of private homes that suddenly changes names to Anthony Road just a quarter mile down. There is a small sign that proclaims "Town Line." What the sign does not readily inform the visitor is that this is also the STATE line and you are now in North Stonington, Connecticut. There are indeed homes that straddle the border, with residence in both states. This has caused quite an unpleasant legal situation which may or may not ever be resolved.

The centerpiece of Ashaway is the Ashaway Free Library located just off Rt. 216 at 15 Knight Street. This library is the quintessential small town library; a small, yet active community resource formally established in 1871.

Assistant librarian, Peggy Roever seems to know everything and everyone. She readily chats up the locals while simultaneously working the computer to find information for a child's school project and checking to see if the latest best seller is available for a village resident. She is friendly, helpful, and eager to share the treasures of this tiny place which run the gamut from book discussion groups to Polaroid camera loans. The library is a wonderful place to capture the very essence of Ashaway, and Roever is a willing and affable guide.

Across from the library at 20 High Street is the home of Joseph Van Den Bossche. It is worth slowing down here and taking a good look at the house because you are taking a good look back into history. The house was built by Jacob D. Babcock in 1778. Babcock was an abolitionist, a fiery man of strong opinions and ideas. During the time of the Underground Railway Babcock and his family hid slaves within this house. Van Den Bossche and his family have owned the property for twenty five years. While the slaves are long gone, the sense of pride in its history remain. Make sure you see this.

There is much for the history buff in Ashaway. The library boasts a bookcase filled chockablock with volumes of Rhode Island and village history. You can explore the background of the Crandall family, find detailed information on the granite quarries that shaped the village, read about the woolen and grist mills of long ago, or about the world famous Ashaway amethyst on milky quartz found here but no longer available.

Holiday time brings The Village Stroll to Ashaway...a time when the entire village comes out to show itself off to the local as well as the tourist. From Breakfast with Santa to craft sales, carriage rides, and an old fashioned carol sing, anyone can find that piece of the road less traveled for themselves.

Top off a visit to the Holiday Stroll with a ride down Old Hopkinton Cemetery Road and Chase Hill Road, where the locals go out of their way to boost the profits of Narragansett Electric (the local power company) yearly. The holiday light displays are almost blinding in their beauty, and some of the individual home decorations, unique. Don't miss it. It's right off Rt. 3... it's an understatement, but... just follow the lights.

The Road To Avondale: 02891

Avondale...if you've lived in the Westerly area for any length of time you know the name. And you know it's somewhere between downtown Westerly and Watch Hill. And you know it's pretty much on the water. And that's probably all you know.

Fact is, Avondale is rich in history. The name "Avondale" first became known in this region in 1893 when Lotteryville, a place on the Pawcatuck River where freights transferred heavy cargoes, petitioned to have its own post office. The Federal Government objected to the name due to local efforts to prohibit gambling. The tiny village complied and submitted three names: Ninigret, Maxtuxet, and Avondale. The name Avondale was chosen for no other reason than the Indian names were difficult to pronounce and spell!

From the docks at Lotteryville an export business in axe handles, hoop poles, and a wide variety of tools thrived. The great gale of 1815 carried one of the Lotteryville docks and a storehouse out to sea. For a long time after, fisherman were bringing up agricultural implements on their lines.

Lotteryville has played a significant part in history. Mr. Potter of Potter Hill, a member of the legislature and director of the Phoenix National and Westerly Savings banks, died at the age of 93. In his will, his nephew J.H. Potter was appointed executor. The latter Mr. Potter found in personal papers a captain's commission from the governor dated May 9, `1814 directing Captain Potter to mobilize his company and immediately march to Lottery Village, "there to meet, expel, and destroy the enemy." This was a more than ambitious project as it meant preventing the British from sending a force up the Pawcatuck River as they lay off Stonington preparing to attack that town. But the story has no end as it is not clear as to what eventually occurred.

In 1848 Ethan Pendleton gave land for a church in Lotteryville. This was significant and of great importance to the times as a peculiarity of the place was a kind of religious hysteria. The Sunday School flourished, and those affected by this kind of hysteria often fell down in a semi-conscious ecstatic state, not an uncommon occurrence for the times.

Fishing was the main industry of Lotteryville's old time families; today the area is dotted with boatyards as you will see in more detail when you take this "road less traveled."

From downtown Westerly follow the Pawcatuck River as Beach Street becomes the Watch Hill Road, or drive out Shore Road and turn left onto the Watch Hill Road. Turn right on Avondale Road, pass the tiny Avondale Chapel built in 1847 but just now getting a new coat of paint, and head for the river, running smack into the Frank Hall Boatyard. As much a part of history as the village itself it joins the Avondale Boatyard and the Lotteryville Marina, circa 1749. The latter marina has made a concession to the 21st Century...it now has a web address carefully embossed on its rustic sign. Boats reign supreme in this tiny slice of New England. They frame a landscape that beckons both the photographer and the dreamer.

Now follow Avondale Road as it curves around the water and back up toward the main road and turn right onto Champlin Drive. Follow Champlin to the end and gaze upon Colonel Willie's Cove. It extends along Champlin Drive near Avondale Village on the southeast side of the drive. It runs out of the Pawcatuck River and up to Lower Avondale Road which connects the tiny Avondale Village with the Watch Hill Road. The interesting thing is that nobody seems to know who Colonel Willie was nor his association with Lotteryville/Avondale. Locals refer to the cove as "Colonel Willies," or even "Colonel's Cove," yet there is evidence in old records of the Westerly Historical Society that at one time it was called Colonel Willet's Cove. Here there was a marsh, which provided a gathering place for Canadian geese, and was popular with fishermen who fished even through the ice in the most severe of winters for smelts.

Talk to an Avondale resident and they might just mention "seining." A seine is a fishing net which hangs vertically in the water, having floats at the upper edge and sinkers at the lower. From the time it was known as Lotteryville this little piece of the area has been known for seining along the Pawcatuck River, especially for striped bass.

Some of the oldest families in the greater Westerly area have their roots in Avondale. Familiar names such as Champlin, Hall, Buffum, Champion, Burdick, Babcock and Rathbun can be found on homes, on mailboxes, and on historical markers within its confines.

When you venture back to the main road, turn right and go into the heart of Watch Hill. Then stop at the newly reopened Olympia Tea Room. Have a light snack or perhaps an elaborate dinner, but make sure you save room for their signature dessert, The Avondale Swan. It's a popular confection named after a place that is truly quintessential New England.

After dinner, drive back one more time to Avondale and take a walk along the river. See the lights from Connecticut winking seductively at you, notice the unique and individual architecture of century old homes, and feel a slight chill on the back of your neck. It might be a breeze off the river, or it might just be Colonel Willie walking the familiar roads of old Lotteryville tapping you on the shoulder and whispering, "Take another look...this is Avondale."

The Road To Bradford: 02808

Most people consider it to be an extension of Westerly. That's partly true because it's a village within the town of Westerly, but still maintains its own fire department and zip code.

Others think it's part of Hopkinton, but they're wrong as well.

And there are some people who say, "Of course I've heard of it, but I'm not really sure where it is."

Welcome to Bradford, Rhode Island. Population approximately 1600 represented by 550 families. A quiet place filled with the noise and memories of a vibrant past.

Bradford is undeniably easy to miss because its land area is just 4 1/2 square miles.

Small, yes. Insignificant, no. Not at all. Consider its history.

Bradford was first named Shattucks Weir (a weir is a fishing dam where nets were set), then it was called Dorrville (after the leader of the Dorr rebellion), and finally Niantic when it was settled several hundred years ago by the Eastern division of the Niantic Indians. The tribe had split into 2 divisions in the 1600s: the Eastern Niantics who settled in southwestern Rhode Island , and the Western Niantics who populated south-central Connecticut. In between, the area was occupied by the Pequot-Mohegan tribes. As allies of the Narragansetts who were based in Charlestown, the Eastern Niantics later merged with the Narragansetts in 1680. The only remaining indication of this birthright is the Niantic Baptist Church on Bowling Lane and Niantic Pizza, a small storefront around the corner from the post office.

Driving into Bradford on Rt. 91 from Hopkinton it is the river you spot first. The Pawcatuck River winds through Bradford, joining together with the Wood River approximately 8 miles upstream. But here in Bradford there is a lovely area just off the road with plenty of parking for those who've come to appreciate the tiny spot.

A woman who identified herself as being "Not from here," eagerly offers, "This is a great place to bring my kids to swim. It's quiet, never crowded, clean, and safe." As if on cue, two children emerge from the river, wrap themselves in towels, shiver for a moment against the early evening air, and disappear into the woman's car. In moments they are gone and the water is still once again.

Parked near the shore is a young man just sitting in his car enjoying the view with his friendly and engaging Rottweiller named Ruby. He firmly declines giving his name but allows that he is a Bradford resident and has been for several years. Does he like living in this peculiar little hamlet?

"Yep. I like it because there aren't too many people here, and I come here to fish. This is the only place around you can launch a boat."

Leaving the river you pull back out onto the road which has now become Main Street. Although years ago Main Street in Bradford was home to a number of businesses, now only Tim Horton Donut Shop, the Bradford Pizza Mart, and a barbershop now remain. The barbershop has, in fact, been in this same location for over 50 years... run for the last 25 years by local, Bill Clachrie.

Quite prominent on Main Street and well known throughout the area is The Jonnycake Center, a service organization that's called Bradford home for more than 28 years. The Jonnycake Center gladly takes in donations of usable clothing and household items and then resells them at rock bottom prices. In addition, the organization provides food baskets and limited funds for utilities and rent for needy families not only Bradford, but in Westerly, Charlestown, and Hopkinton as well.

Turn off Main Street and onto Bowling Lane, and you encounter a study in contrasts. On the corner is a social club. On the side of the building is the sign, "Bradford Social Club," but any resident will tell you that this is "just The Social Club. The real Bradford Social Club is on Woody Hill Road, just a little way aways. It used to be the Bocce Club and is now known as The Citizens Club. This club was for the Italian population that worked the quarries in Bradford, and The Social Club was for the English residents who were in the Bradford Dye Mill. For such a small population, Bradford sure is sociable! The clubs are "members only" organizations with little more than a bar and a place to have a party, but to the local residents this is their local gathering place.

At 70 Bowling Lane the Neighborhood Center works hard to serve not only as a social center for the youth of Bradford, but also as an after-school venue where kids ae helped with homework, where they can come for help, and just for moral support and guidance.

Neighborhood gathering places in Bradford are as simple as the front stoop. On summer evenings nearly everyone on Bowling Lane is sitting out front; often whole families spanning several generations. Each car that drives down the road gets full scrutiny; every person walking by is either greeted out of familiarity, or stared at because they are unknown to the residents.

Bowling Lane's homes are a study in contrast as you go from one end of the street to the other. At the start of the road by the social club, and for most of Bowling Lane, the homes are modest duplexes, many in need of a new paint job or a new roof. Yet there is fierce pride in ownership. Lawns are neatly mowed, flowers are carefully planted, and at #34 Bowling Lane there is a handmade tribute to the brave firefighters of September 11th. Adorning the front lawn is a well made replica of the statue of the New York City firemen planting the flag at Ground Zero. It is well done, and well worth your time to view it.

Drive to the end of the road and suddenly a mansion appears on your left side, rising up high on the horizon to greet the visitor. This is #120, and the home for the last 41 years of Ray and Juliette Piccolo, a charming couple who enjoy talking about Bradford and showing off their home.

Their sons Ray and Bradley were hard at work in the yard, having come from Ft. Lauderdale and Coral Springs, Florida respectively to help paint their parents' home for "just a few days."

"Yes," laughed Ray, "We came for a few days and we've been here for 4 weeks! We power washed, we painted, we did lawn work, and it's still not all done, but it is a beautiful house, isn't it?"

Indeed it is. The home, which was built in 1924, was originally the home of the owner of the Bradford Dye Association. It is massive in size with a slate roof, a tennis court in the backyard, and a large amount of square footage. Years ago when the mill thrived, the various owner/ managers would live in this house; across the road middle management occupied other upscale homes. And the mill workers lived at the other end of the road, in the more modest housing. At the time most of these people were immigrants from England and Ireland, having been brought to Rhode Island by the company which originally was located in Bradford, England. The company quickly grew to dominate the tiny town of Niantic, and the name was subsequently changed to Bradford.

When the mill thrived, Bradford thrived. Just ask James Cofone, an 81 year resident of the town. "Bradford was lively in those days. We had two A & Ps, a pharmacy, Grills Bar, my father ran Cofone's Grocery, and the train always stopped here for freight to the plant and also for the people. Douglas Park was at the very top of the 'The Lane,'...that's what they called Bowling Lane back then. There was a big ball field there and always something going on. We had carnivals and circuses...it was beautiful."

Cofone blamed the depression for the downward turn for Bradford Dye, or BDA as it was known to the locals.

"When BDA went downhill," said Cofone, "So did the town. Then supermarkets came into the picture in Westerly and that kind of squeezed out the little grocery stores. Competition set in to the textile industry during the depression; and like Fall River and New Bedford, the mills suffered. Work went to the southern part of the country because labor was cheaper."

Still Cofone is optimistic about Bradford. "They are trying to appropriate money to pave the streets, to put in more sidewalks, to get home improvement loans. I give them credit. Little by little it's happening."

Juliette Piccolo echoes Cofone's optimism. She has lived in Bradford for 80 years, save for 5 years during World War II when she and husband Ray lived in Bridgeport, Connecticut. "But I came back," she says, "To Bradford. It's my home...isn't it beautiful?"

The Road to Carolina: 02812

Like a tiny baguette that's barely noticed on a larger piece of jewelry, Carolina sits on the edge of the town of Richmond and also on the edge of the town of Charlestown, waiting to be explored by the traveler who likes to dig and look just a bit deeper to get to the essence of a place.

The Carolina postal clerk in the phone booth of a post office on Rt. 91, just off Rt. 112, tells us that while she's not sure of the exact population of the village, she has 245 box holders and 345 rural delivery customers who use 02812 as their Carolina zip code. And yet fringes of the village extend into two other zip codes.

Certainly the geographic identity of the place is sketchy. Although the post office is in the town of Charlestown, it is both Richmond and Charlestown that claim Carolina as their own. The town of Richmond was originally a part of Charlestown, incorporated in 1747. It was named for Edward Richmond, the Attorney General of the colony from 1671 to 1680 who took an active part of the original settlement of the area.

Like many other Washington County communities 17th Century Richmond was home for many early settlers. After purchasing land from the Indians, these wealthy Narragansett planters who were intelligent and well educated settled in South County and made Richmond the wealthiest area in Rhode Island for many years.

Although the end of the plantation era signaled the beginning of the early water-power industry which furnished power for its sawmills and textile industry, Richmond was still largely a rural area and remains so to this day. More than 60 percent of the town is undeveloped woodland, and only small villages dot the landscape. Like Carolina.

The boundaries of Carolina are not well defined. Coming from Charlestown north on Rt. 112 you run into Carolina without really being aware of it , somewhere near the Charlestown Middle School . Carolina then turns sharply left onto Rt. 91 toward Westerly while continuing north on Rt. 112 to the Town of Richmond sign... and then beyond. And yet when you reach the Washington County Fairgrounds you're told you're in Wyoming, yet another part of Richmond. It's a rich tapestry that makes up Carolina's geography, and an even richer one that makes up its history.

Just ask John Quinn, a self-styled "Mayor of Main Street" whose family has been in Carolina appreciating their good fortune for seven generations.

"My great-great grandfather came from Ireland to be taken in by relatives in Boston, which is what the Irish in Boston did back then," laughed Quinn. "The story goes that on the way to Boston my great-great grandfather got lost and wound up in Carolina. He was too damned stubborn to admit it, so he stayed, married, and had 13 kids! He had a farm and 10 of those kids grew to adulthood, helping on the farm. The girls worked in the mill, and most of them married managers and owners of the mill. Thus the mill became part of my family's life."

Quinn, a retired newspaperman who worked at the Providence Journal for 23 years and then became an editor with USA Today in Rochester and Washington, D.C., moved around alot, but always kept coming back to Carolina because it was home base for his family.

In the 1980s the man who owned the mill property at the time died and left 32 derelict, crumbling buildings. Quinn and his sons heard about this and decided to make a trip back to Carolina to look over the property.

"It was just before Mother's Day," said Quinn, "and the price was right. One of my sons said, "Let's buy it for mother."

So they did, and John Quinn's wife became "the slum lady of Carolina" he recounts with great relish.

Thus the Quinns went to work and began refurbishing, cleaning up, and rebuilding the mill buildings into a family compound. Today nearly half of the original mill buildings have been restored and the Quinns, their children, and grandchildren live in them. They have, as the centerpiece of the mill, a family center that is used both by them and by the community in the summer. "From the local Rotary Club to the Preservation Society fundraiser, we make our family center available for community activities."

The fervor started by the Quinns has become contagious. Many Carolina neighbors pitched in to clean up the decay and make their village beautiful.

One of the famous landmarks that makes many a head turn while driving by is The Octagon House located at the junction of Richmond Townhouse Road, Shannock Hill Road, Pine Hill Road, and Main Street. Purchased by the Carolina Preservation Society it has likewise been refurbished and is being used for community activities serving communities from Westerly to Richmond.

"The strength of this community is its longtime residents," offers Quinn. People like Bill Grimes who built a beautiful little park next to his auto body shop, people like Vetta Scudder, whose homestead was built in 1784 by John Hoxsie and still stands, or Dick Wolke, a retired URI Professor and President of the Richmond Historic Society, or Virginia Woodmansee who's lived in

RONA MANN

Carolina 59 years because 'It's such a pretty little village,' or just plain good neighbors like Charles and Hazel Dyson or Vetta Scudder... these are the people who shape Carolina."

And that's what makes this "road less traveled" special. At first blush you could just drive through and never notice it, but stop, pull over, and talk to a few of the people. As Vetta Scudder will tell you, "It's always been such a self-respecting little town."

Carolina is rich in its past ,and even richer for the people who today work to shape its future.

The Road to: Clarks Falls 06359

Across from a farm on Rt. 216 in Clarks Falls five cows are lying down lazily munching the grass on a warm day in June. One lone cow in their midst is standing , looking out at the horizon. If you believe the old adage that when cows lie down it's going to rain, then this bovine standing proudly must indeed be the optimist of the herd.

How fitting then that the cow was standing in a field in Clarks Falls, Connecticut, a mere blip on the map, but a tiny corner of southern New England that is filled with the wonder of its past and a blatant optimism for its future. That's not just opinion; that's fact. Just ask the people who live there!

Anna Coit was born in Clarks Falls and has no intention of moving. Anna knows every corner of the tiny hamlet. Together with her sister they founded the Walter Palmer Society. Palmer was one of the original settlers in the village and has, according to Coit, "Thousands of descendants. Last we knew it was over 22,600! There's even a monument to him in Wequetequock Cemetery."

Coit continues, "Clarks Falls is in a technical glacial valley. The glacier came down and we ended up with a pile of glacial till with a stream on each side. There are also a lot of glacial sinkholes caused by lumps of ice partially covered by soil. As a result we have some beautiful hollows here."

There are several ways to get to this pastoral village. From Rt. 3 in Ashaway drive north to the Hopkinton General Store in Hopkinton City and turn left onto Clarks Falls Road. Drive less than a mile, cross the state line, and you've arrived. From Exit 93 off I-95 turn onto Rt. 216 North, pass the truck stop and proceed down the country road. Cross the Green Fall ("There's no 's' on Green Fall," chides Anna Coit) River and step into history as you gaze upon Clarks Falls Grist Mill, the oldest industry in the original town of Stonington. The grist mill is owned today by John Palmer, a dairy farmer who lives in the area. Although everything is "just as it was," according to village residents, the grist mill is not active at present and many wonder if Palmer has any interest in maintaining it.

The town of North Stonington contained many districts and settlements in the 1800s. Most had a school, a church, and a post office. Some had stores. Often these villages developed around a mill to take advantage of its water power. Such is the case with Clarks Falls. The little village post office, however, was the last one to close in 1947 following the lead of Laurel Glen, Pendleton Hill, and Ashwillet, other small settlements within the town of North Stonington. When it was opened it thrived as part of E.P. Chapman's store, a place where one could find anything from elixirs to penny candy. The last postmistress, Gladys Walter, still lives in Clarks Falls. For those not able to frequent the store in person, Ernest Chapman rode around in a horse and buggy taking customers' orders. When the orders were filled, he delivered them. And the people who lived there then still live there now in latter day incarnations. The Clarkes . . . The Palmers . . . The Perrys ...The Bills. Children and children's children seem captivated by this jewel of a village and see no reason to move.

Edwin C. Bill was born in 1918. "My family were all born before there was a Westerly Hospital, so they were born at the family homestead." Bill bought the homestead for himself in 1942 and built onto it. He still lives there...sees no reason to move. "My son did move away," he offers with a smile in his voice. "He lives 3 miles up in the road in Laurel Glen."

If you follow Rt. 216 it stops at the famous "corners" in Clarks Falls where Clarks Falls Rd. meets Dennison Hill Road and then takes a turn. Rt. 216 ends at Pendleton Hill Road and the junction of Boom Bridge Road. A little back from the road on the hillside is the John E. Clark homestead. For 37 years Clark was the proprietor of the saw and grist mills at Clarks Falls, retiring in 1875.

In 1919 the Clark's daughter and her husband, John B. Perry moved into the old homestead and spent the rest of their lives in that home. John Perry was a teacher, a Grange member, and for a time wrote for the Westerly Sun under the caption , "Birchen Mills."(the name for the village pond before it became known as Clark's Falls Pond).

Across Boom Bridge Road from the Clark homestead is a plot of land that runs to Spalding Pond known as "Iron Works Pasture." The iron works of Dr. Asa Spalding were located here many years hence. Dr. Thurman P. Maine owned a home at Spalding Pond and had nine children. While Maine died many years ago, his children still all live in Clarks Falls and according to Anna Coit, "They don't wait for a yearly reunion; they get together once a month for a party! Anniversaries, birthdays, they're very close and are always celebrating something together."

The Green Fall River, which rises in Voluntown, formerly passed east of the Birchen Mill Pond and united with waters a little below the road leading east to Hopkinton City. When a factory was erected in 1861encompassing a saw, grist, and bark mill all in one, the owners divided the waters from its natural bed and diverted it into what is now known as Clark's Falls Pond. This furnished the power needed for the factory.

The heart of Clark's Falls is the four corners. No matter to whom you speak they keep referring you back to the four corners. From here you may proceed 1 mile north to Laurel Glen, another tiny village with major roots to the past. You can go west to more developed parts of North Stonington, south on 216 to the Interstate, or east to Hopkinton City in Rhode Island. Each direction proves an adventure, from the well kept old homesteads, to the sprawling working farms, to the ghosts where once stood the mills, Chapman's store, the post office, and the shadows of lives lived long ago.

This is Clark's Falls...just a name on an exit sign, a small quadrant drawn on a map, and an enduring source of pride for the families who live there.   J. Allison Bill, a lifelong resident and farmer until his retirement put it best when he said about his hometown, "It's open...completely open. You can live here and no one will bother you."

No wonder then as we turned right onto Clark's Falls Road and headed for Rt. 3 in Hopkinton that cow was still standing, looking optimistically out over the landscape even though it had begun to rain.

RONA MANN

The Road To: Cross Mills 02813

Right off the bat we find a great difference of opinion just in the name itself. Some say "Cross Mills." Others make it a possessive by spelling it "Cross' Mills." And still others both pronounce and spell it "Crosses Mills." Not wishing to incite the wrath of either local or native, we'll call it Cross Mills because that's what the state painted on the sign.

And that sign is designated a Charlestown exit off Rt. 1. It's the same exit the traveler takes for the Breachway or Charlestown Beach. And it also serves as the official marker for Cross Mills.

Cross Mills, which for many years was surrounded by farms and served as the center of Charlestown, is really nothing more today than a neighborhood, but what a diverse and wonderful little conclave it is!

First, a history lesson. Joseph Cross, the son of John Cross who settled in the colony in the late 1600s, inhabited this area on the Old Post Road near the junction of routes 1 and 2 and began running a grist mill in 1709. For many years this was the only village in the area. Cross' Mill was a mill for grinding Indian corn, and later in the 1700s the Cross family had a blacksmith shop adjacent to the mill. Today if you drive to the crossroads of Rt. 2 and Old Post Road there remains the stone foundation and spillway and dam of the Cross' Grist Mill on the north side of the road on Cross' Mill Pond. This mill pond goes underneath the road and into the brook to the salt pond. The foundation of the early Cross house can be seen by climbing the old stone steps where the house stood on the crest of a small hill. By the early 1930s the house was empty and rotting so the Cross Mills Fire Department set it afire as a practice drill since the home was beyond habitation or repair.

The Cross family was very community minded. Local historians have record of Peleg, a son of Joseph Cross, serving on the town council when the village of Cross Mills became Charlestown.

His son, Peleg II followed in his father's footsteps on the town council after serving as a colonel in the American Revolution. Descendants of the original Cross family remained active in town government through the twentieth century.

Benjamin Gavitt followed the Cross tradition by grinding Indian corn for "jonny cake" meal in the local grist mill, and coincidentally was also prominent in town affairs. In the early part of the twentieth century Gavitt's grist mill and his Jonny Cake Meal were much sought after by both the locals and those who traveled miles to purchase this famous product. Gavitt was also responsible for establishing the first volunteer Fire Department in Cross Mills and served as the village's first fire chief when a larger department was later built.

18

Today's Cross Mills reflects change, but is still deeply rooted in its past. It's an art gallery, an excavating business, it's real estate, and dockage for boats large and small; and at the heart and soul of this tiny hamlet is The Cross' Mills Library, the centerpiece of the community.

The library was built in 1913 by the Cross Mills Baptist Church library association from the proceeds of a lawn party. The new building set them back $627.05 and opened with just 500 books on their shelves.

With quick financial support from the state as well as the Town of Charlestown the library was able to progress from kerosene lights and wood heat to electric lights and many more books.

Today the Cross' Mills Public Library boasts thousands of books, ongoing community programs, and is fully equipped with computers.

The Charlestown Historical Society operates from this location and oversees the District 2 Schoolhouse which sits on common land and dates back to 1838. It is still used today for tours and meetings.

It would be impossible to speak about Cross Mills without mention of its Native American history. Fort Ninigret, a Niantic Indian site just south of the library is an historic site dating back to the seventeenth century. The Niantics were closely related to the Narragansett Indians who controlled almost the whole of Rhode Island in the early 1700s. Their fort is situated on a bluff facing the breachway and barrier beach at the northern end of Ninigret Salt Pond.

The most prominent feature at Fort Ninigret is a rectangular earth and stone embankment with 5-sided bastions at three of the four corners. Local archaeological speculation over the builders of this earthwork and its date of origin causes controversy. One theory actually speculates construction between 700 and 1300 A.D. with actual occupation in the 17th century.

An important activity at Fort Ninigret was the manufacture of Indian shell beads or wampum which was used as a kind of currency.

It may surprise, but Fort Ninigret was not ever intensely occupied by the Native Americans. There appear to be only a few fireplaces within the area, and no large storage or refuse areas associated with ongoing occupancy. Artifacts that have been discovered indicate that fishing and the collecting of oysters were popular activities necessary for life sustenance, as well as the practice of agriculture.

When we embarked upon the road less traveled to Cross Mills or Cross' Mills or Crosses Mills depending upon your preference, we started with the history of the place. And yet it is impossible to end the history lesson and move on, because that's the very thing about history. It

RONA MANN

isn't necessarily old or stagnant or confined to the past. By its very nature history continues, it thrives, and it constantly changes. Take a drive and find your history on the road to Cross Mills.

The Road To: Enders Island 06355

It came as a suggestion from an anonymous reader.

The idea was later reinforced by a Hopkinton neighbor.

The suggestion and the reinforcement fed natural curiosity, and it eventually led to a road not taken...the road to Enders Island, Connecticut.

If you're wondering if you've somehow missed a local island with a great beach, fried clam shacks, and souvenir stores filled with pretty shells, guess again. Enders Island is the antithesis of all that.

It is quiet. It is beautiful. And there doesn't appear to even be a place to buy a Coke. Welcome to the end of a winding road and the beginning of a beautiful adventure.

You venture toward Mystic, but never really reach the village. You turn off onto Masons Island Road and wend your way past the boat liveries and any suggestion of tourist activity.

In a short while the road veers to the right, there are almost no more cars in view, the landscape turns from one of boats crammed side by side, to beautiful sprawling homes on well landscaped acres. To your left is the Long Island Sound with sailboats silently skimming the water. Now follow the signs to Enders Island...to a world just up the road, yet far removed from the one you just left behind.

Walking along the road are Claire and Edward Welshock. Although they live in the area and this view could be taken for granted, they appear to never stop appreciating the opportunity to walk amidst such breathtaking surroundings. Claire works just up the road at the Saint Edmund's Retreat on Enders Island. When asked what is so special about St. Edmund's she replies, "Just go up there and see for yourself. People have been reborn there."

So up the road the traveler ventures. Past more homes, more flowers, even a tree in the middle of the road. The road takes you across a breakwater at the southeast end of Masons Island, and suddenly you've arrived. There is no neon welcome sign, no fried clam shack, no public beach. What does welcome the traveler, however, is a 12 acre island situated on the south entrance to Mystic Bay; and most prominent, indeed swallowing up the entire island, is The Society of Saint Edmund Monastery and Retreat House.

RONA MANN

The Society of Saint Edmund is a clerical religious congregation whose priests and brothers consecrated to follow Jesus Christ, share a common life, and keep vows of chastity, poverty, and obedience.

Their essential mission is evangelization, with their principal works dedicated to African American ministry, Catholic education, spiritual renewal, and pastoral ministry.

It is the spiritual renewal that pervades Enders Island and the lush property on which are housed a chapel, retreat house, and institute of sacred art.

Walking the property you are struck by the absolute quiet of the place. People pass by with a smile or a nod, boats skim the nearby waters, a young woman is poised with easel erect and paint brush in hand recording the moment, the air is redolent with the scent of flowering shrubs, a couple reclines on chaise lounges with books in hand, and everywhere it is so very, very quiet.

Judy and Joe Drenga from St. Joseph's Church in Vernon, Connecticut are here for the week, for a retreat and renewal of the spirit. It is not their first time on Enders Island; it will not be their last, they say. They urge the visitor to go inside the brand new chapel, made possible by a generous donation from a Stonington resident.

Once inside, "awesome" takes on its proper meaning. It is a simple beauty that astounds. In a small room off to the side is a memorial to Saint Edmund of Canterbury, with his hand perfectly preserved and encased in glass. The actual chapel itself is tiny, but there is a warmth and a feeling here that cannot be described. Theologians have written about the beauty of holiness. Here there is a holiness of beauty.

Leaving the island, the car radio intrudes, breaking the mood; and someone on a talk station somewhere is babbling mindlessly about travel. Suddenly there's a pause, and the voice on the radio says, "I don't have to go far away when I travel. It just has to feel far away."

Welcome to Enders Island, Connecticut.

The Road To: Greenhaven 06379

If you've lived in this area for any time at all you've no doubt driven by the Wequetequock Fire Department on Rt. 1 in Stonington, Connecticut a number of times. And maybe that's all you did, just drive on by; but if you stop next time and take the "road less traveled," you'll be in for a real treat for both the amateur historian and the lover of nature that lies within so many of us.

When you reach the Wequetequock Fire Department, turn left at the traffic light. You're now on Greenhaven Road. Take an immediate right again onto Palmer Neck Road, and step back into history...a history that helped to shape the very founding of the town of Stonington.

Immediately on your left is the Wequetequock Burial Grounds, dating back to 1650. Park your vehicle and get out...this one's worth more than a passing glance! Also known as the Stonington Founders' Cemetery it serves as the final resting place for the first four families in Stonington: The Palmers, the Chesebroughs, the Stantons, and the Minors. While burial there used to be limited to just the descendants of these four families, now you can become a "friend" of the cemetery through the historical society; and as such you can hobnob with the founding families when your time comes.

After exploring the small cemetery and taking photos of graves that date back as far as Walter Palmer's wolf stone with its inscription of "Born: 1585 and Died: 1661", continue driving down Palmer Neck Road until you reach #146. The mailbox with the number is on the left side of the road, but you cannot miss the home itself situated on the right. And make sure you bring your camera. #146 Palmer Neck Road is owned by one Al Hartunian, a 71 year old gentleman with a love of architecture and design, who has his tongue more than firmly planted in his cheek.

Hartunian's father bought this parcel of land in 1937 and kept it in the family until 1963 when Al himself built a small four room home as a summer house. After that, however, according to Hartunian who was delighted to have an opportunity to talk about his home, "I just added and added some more." The "some more" amounts to about 3000 square feet, ten rooms, and even a small chapel on the inside of the house. But the real story is on the outside...and you have only to put on your directional and pull over to see what we mean.

At first glance you see a castle...but then you see more and more and more. A tower, turrets, gargoyles; and a scarecrow with the face of Ray Bolger!

"I had to get a variance from the town when I started building the tower, "offers Hartunian, " But that involved permission from only one neighbor and he knew I was just having a good time, so he didn't block it."

The stone tower has stained glass windows, and the gargoyles go completely around to the back of the house. Inside, the tower is all brick; outside it's all stone.

"It's constant," Hartunian went on, "The people coming to look, but I don't mind. I'm glad they enjoy what I've done."

And in truth, he's done all the work himself with no architectural background. When he retired he owned a laundromat and some apartments. When he saw how expensive his project was getting he called upon his own resources, knocking on doors in Lisbon, Connecticut for example, to pick stones for the front wall and drives.

"A woman told me she'd charge me $2. per truckload. I knew that was a deal, so I just made 50 truckload pickups. And can you imagine", Hartunian went on, "Someone actually rang my bell one day and asked if we rented out the yard for weddings?"

Yes...we can.

Leaving the Hartunian homestead continue down Greenhaven Road through the curves over a narrow bridge and past the "End of Town Road" sign. Although the road turns rough, the adventure is about to begin! Welcome to the Barn Island Wildlife Management Area, maintained by the Division of Environmental Protection, State of Connecticut. Bring your insect repellant, your binoculars, and your sense of adventure as you park your car on the right and encounter the trail head.

Spring is the perfect time to explore Barn Island Wildlife Management as the ospreys plan their return. You will no doubt also encounter members of the heron family as you head east through the gate by a memorial stone and onto a wide trail. Follow the trail across 700 acres of salt marshes, separated here and there by woodland. Follow the faintly marked trails as they wind and curve until you are back to your starting place. The water directly in front of you beckons you to turn your attention to this quintessential New England scene, but the sign cautions your loitering for long: "Restricted for fishing and launching of boats."

The fishes of this tidal marsh are noted by signs: bluefish, winter flounder, Atlantic Silversiders, and Mummichogs. These are spawning, nursery, and feeding areas, and some of the most beautiful around situated in a very secluded and peaceful spot.

Walk back to your car, turn around, go back down Palmer Neck Road to the beginning of Greenhaven and turn right. For the next couple of miles your ride is unremarkable; homes liberally dot your landscape on both sides of the street. When Greenhaven Road ends, pause for a moment at the right fork. This is the home of Davis Farm, established in 1654 and well known in these parts for their cider mill, hay rides, and especially their registered Belgian horses. The Davis Farm's horse and team are rented out frequently for everything from wedding receptions to parades and events in Rhode Island and Connecticut.

To your left is River Road, a lovely ride that takes you along a good length of the Pawcatuck River with boatyards and marinas quite plentiful on your right and private homes on the left. Give more than a passing glance to #370 River Road. In their front yard is a large rock. Perched atop the rock and yet seemingly quite secure, are Adirondack chairs, bringing to mind how peaceful it must be to sit "on top of the world" on a warm summer's day, sipping a lemonade or adult beverage and enjoying the sprawling river view.

(Robert L. Smith, owner of the home, subsequently informed us that there is a sign leading up to that rock. "It is titled MARTINI POINT and has been since I bought the house in 1988.")

Go through the STOP sign at Mary Hall Road. The road now becomes Mechanic Street and suddenly you're back into the busy world of Davis Standard, Cottrell Brewing, and many other small businesses and offices in downtown Pawcatuck. Your adventure has ended for today, but best of all is the knowledge that just a few miles in back of you lie the monuments of centuries past, the promise of spring in the birds' return, and the gargoyles and turrets and towers of someone with a vivid imagination and a sense of whimsy who built something for you to enjoy... just down the road.

The Road To Hillsdale: 02898

It seems so many of these "road" stories center on old mill villages. But such is the very foundation that built this area. It was primarily the mills that created the economy that in turn built these surrounding towns.

And this is indeed the case with the tiny burg of Hillsdale. "Where?" you ask. Never heard of it? Don't feel bad. Most people haven't. Fact is, Hillsdale never had a big presence in our area in the past, and has even less of one now; yet the Hillsdale of years past was a viable place found right in the heart of the town of Richmond, perhaps a mile north of Route 138. Beaver River, which powered the old mill, runs alongside it, flowing into a small pond.

The remains of the factory that thrived during the Civil War are barely visible. The factory manufactured Army blankets and denim trousers to be sold in the South. Like so many area mills, fire destroyed it, but it was rebuilt soon after and continued to operate until after the War ended.

Just south, along the river, was an old grist mill which ground Indian corn into meal. It also burned, was revived as a shingle mill, burned down yet again, and was never rebuilt.

The centerpiece of Hillsdale as it exists today is the Beaver River Preserve, some 241 acres of forested wetland, a mixed oak forest, a bog pool, swamp, a high quality trout stream, and undisturbed flora and fauna.

Hikers may enjoy two trails, one of which runs from Hillsdale Road west to the bog. Bring along a net...the rare bog copper butterfly is plentiful here, along with many species of dragonflies.

People who live in Hillsdale have lived here a long time, but not all are natives. Local business owner Brad Friel moved to Hillsdale 33 years ago, buying the country home of his then father-in-law, Roger Braman. Braman's home had originally been the site of the Masonic Men's Club, but the North Kingstown resident had purchased it as a country getaway. Friel bought it from him and kicked it up a notch.

Today Friel's property is known as Willow Valley Farm. His daughter, Alison Ward runs the farm. Another daughter, Amy raises and trains horses there. It is a sprawling, well-cared for piece of property with its roots deeply entrenched in the history of the surrounding land.

"When I first moved here," Friel offers, "There were nothing but dirt roads. Now look at it."

Look at it, indeed. Hillsdale Road is hardly a mecca of suburban sprawl. There is not a single commercial business along the road. There are no traffic lights, no restaurants, and few signs.

The Village was originally called Kenyon's Factory, named for Whitman Kenyon who operated one of the original mills. One of his sons, Alfred went on to serve as tax collector, assessor, town councilor, State Representative in 1863, and finally State Senator in 1875, subsequently serving 8 terms. It was his legislation in part that won the appropriation to create the courthouse that stands in West Kingston to this day.

Just south of the village, off Hillsdale Road is Punchbowl Road, named for the Punchbowl School, an old schoolhouse of which only the foundation remains. Punchbowl refers to a very deep round hole just feet from the foundation and near Hillsdale Road. Locals have also nicknamed it Devil's Punchbowl and Indian Punchbowl. The school is now gone, but Punchbowl Road with its lively history and legends extends all the way from Hillsdale to Usquepaugh.

Local residents also tell the story of the town pound. More than 250 years ago a pound was built for animals who often strayed. Unlike today when a stray is merely a nuisance or a likely victim of traffic, years ago animals were looked upon as necessary for work. Therefore a wandering head of livestock could seriously affect a family's financial situation, not to mention their very survival. Hillsdale history boasts records dating back as far as 1752 showing the election of a Pound Keeper, considered a position of vital importance for the times.

The intersection at Punchbowl School is called Bailey Hill Road in one direction and Bailey Hill Trail in the other, the latter connecting to Carolina Nooseneck Road which will eventually bring the traveler back to Rt. 138. The Bailey roads were named for the descendants of S.B. Bailey who lived in Hillsdale close to 300 years ago. One of these descendants, Richard Bailey, was Richmond's first town moderator in 1747.

Across the road from the mill pond is the prized De Coppett Estate, Theakston De Coppett moved from New York in the early 1900s, purchased this property, and built a massive two-story home on the land. De Coppett was one of Rhode Island's earliest conservationists and kept purchasing surrounding property until more than 2500 acres had been accumulated at the time of his death in 1935. His will bequeathed all of it to the state, which today still owns and maintains it as a reservation and sanctuary.

So... Hillsdale will never be much more than it is right now, and that's just fine with the people who quietly inhabit its land. The mills have long since stopped operating and were never rebuilt. The roads have been paved, but not for the creation of shopping centers. And a very wise man years ago saw fit to buy the land he so loved and provide for its preservation, so that in the future when one might embark upon the "road less traveled" in Hillsdale, Rhode Island, one would find it the way it was, hearing little more along the way than echoes of the past.

The Road To: Hope Valley 02832

It barely has its own identity. Going north on I-95 it shares the exit sign with Alton. Going south it shares an exit with Rt. 138 East towards Newport.

People in South County kind of know where it is, but many aren't real certain. They know that that's the place with the bakery that makes those delicious bismarcks, but few know even the name of the bakery. People up north either confuse it with the town of Hope located between Coventry and Scituate, or remember " going down there once to the Enchanted Forest or to get a Christmas tree." But they can't really place it and " sure don't know much about it."

But the people in Hope Valley don't mind at all. They even chuckle over it. They don't want too many people to find them...they like Hope Valley just the way it is.

Although the tee shirts and sweatshirts that hang in the window at Ma And Pa's Country Store proclaim, "Hope Valley: Best Little Town in Rhode Island," Hope Valley isn't a town at all, but a village within the town of Hopkinton.

The village is home to approximately 1446 people, some of whom are people from "up north" who wanted a bigger home for less money and didn't mind the commute to work, while others are dyed-in-the-wool "swamp yankees"...folks who were born here, live here, rarely venture from here, and plan on dying here.

You can reach Hope Valley from the Westerly/Pawcatuck area either by taking I-95 North to Exit 2, or by taking the slower, more scenic route...Rt. 3 North from downtown Westerly through Ashaway, into Hopkinton City, and finally into Hope Valley.

Rt. 3 winds through farmland and residential property, taking you up the hill from the Wood River Health Center, a first rate family clinic, and then down the hill past The Fenner Hill Golf Club with its challenging course and popular year round restaurant.

If you've got kids in the car and the weather's warm and the season's in full swing stop at The Enchanted Forest, a delightful way to pass a few hours of amusement. Now come down the steep hill past homes with decades of history and you're into "downtown" Hope Valley.

Don't blink, as the saying goes, or you'll miss it! Hope Valley is one of the few places left in America that doesn't have a traffic light. It has a blinking light down at the bottom of the hill where Rt. 3 meets Spring Street (Rt. 138 west towards Connecticut). There is a traffic light about 3/4 of a mile ahead, but by then you're in Wyoming...and that's another place with another story for another time.

So there you are at the blinking light. To your left is The Spring Street Market. Every tiny town in America's got a "Spring Street Market." It's a convenience store- pizza takeout- movie rental- fried chicken shack -lottery ticket outlet all in one. The floors are wooden slats that creak when customers bustle in and out; the place is tiny, but it has a personality and an obvious history.

And while you're at the blinker pull your car into the lot of "that bakery with the bismarcks." It's West's Bakery; and in addition to the confections for which they're famous, they serve breakfast, lunch, and have a late night ice cream window in the summer. In the morning it's the place to find every contractor, politician, and well-known in the village. The trucks line the parking lot, while inside the conversation is lively; and yes, they do look up when a stranger comes in.

Across from West's is the Fire Department, the touchstone of Hope Valley. There's always something going on at the firehouse whether it's a craft show, a demonstration, or an open house. The volunteer firemen are serious about what they do, enjoy teaching children and showing off the equipment, and pointing with pride to their well manicured station, ably run by Chief Fred Stanley. And of course there's a framed photograph in front, and a sign that proclaims, "Home of Billy Gilman."(he's the adolescent singer who has rocked the world of country music in recent years and a native of these parts).

Follow the road a bit further into downtown and discover more hidden treasures in this historic village. The Hack and Livery Shop brings tourists as well as locals for everything from candy in the barrel to antiques. It is a welcoming attraction with a large parking lot and bears a visit; or if it's been years since you've gone and poked around, another trip.

URE Outfitters on the left side of the road takes up a lot of space, both outside and in. It's a curious place for the outdoorsman with everything from camping equipment to fishing paraphernalia to knives to clothing to hunting outfits. It's the kind of store that you can return to many times and never see it all. And the advice and help are good, free, and accurate!

Hope Valley is the home of antique shops, of consignment shops, of shops that come and go according to the business climate, but their patronage is comprised of the loyal swamp yankees and small town converts who have discovered the village and made it their own.

On the right hand side of the street is Dow Field, the official home of the Chariho Little League and busy constantly from early spring to late fall. The fence is lined with advertising from businesses as far away as Westerly who obviously know the value of stands consistently filled with spectators.

Across the street from Dow Field is the Wyoming Fruit and Vegetable Company, which at first blush is just a roadside stand; but ask any of the locals and they'll tell you different. Seems that owner Bruce Bryant, and his mother Joyce have operated this business for the last 27 years.

They generally open for the season just before Palm Sunday and work their way through seasonal plants, annuals, perennials, fruits, and vegetables right up to the sale of Christmas trees, after which they close down for a couple of months. Bruce is known for his yellow labrador retrievers that are more white in color than yellow. The pride of the stand was "Lil" who succumbed to cancer just a few years ago, but left her legacy in D.O.L.(daughter of Lil) or Dolly as everyone calls her. Along the way there have been other dogs, but it is Lil's portrait in oils that hangs proudly over the string beans and apples at Bruce's place and the one the locals remember for always hanging around, ready to beg for food from any customer. When no customers were around, Lil would wend her way up the road into Wyoming and "knock" on the back door of the village pizza place, where she was often rewarded with lasagna.

Once you pull out of Wyoming Fruit and Vegetable you're out of Hope Valley. The sign for "Richmond" is just past Bruce's driveway, so turn around, because you're not through with Hope Valley yet.

Drive back on Main Street to the blinking light at the bakery, this time turning right onto Spring Street (Rt. 138 West). Drive up for about a mile and a half passing the popular Whispering Pines Campground on your right. Shortly past the campground turn right onto Woody Hill Road. This is a great ride!

Woody Hill Road is aptly named. It is well wooded and you twist and turn through the curves, going up and down a series of small, scenic hills. WJJF Radio, the brainchild of John Fuller and a welcome country music presence in the area is on your right, housed in little more than a quonset hut that also is home to Fuller Printing.

Horses graze contentedly here and there along Woody Hill Road, and homes dot the landscape, ranging from simple farms to elaborate domiciles. The road goes for miles and ends finally at Rt. 165 in Voluntown, Connecticut. Turn left onto Rt. 165, notice the places advertising trail rides, and continue for perhaps a couple of miles. You'll see the junction of Rt. 138 and you'll want to turn left, back onto Spring Street. The ride goes for about 5 or 6 miles taking you past more farms, homes, a craft shop, Camp Yawgoog (the Boy Scout camp), a French furniture barn, and then finally there's that blinking light and you're back. Back in the little village that manages in just a small amount of space to have bismarcks and camping equipment and baseball and consignment stores and flowers and vegetables, and most of all, wonderful hometown people who have pride in all that's theirs...even the memory of a white dog begging shamelessly for all she was worth.

RONA MANN

The Road To Hopkinton City: 02833

Hopkinton can be confusing to the uninitiated who have never jumped in a vehicle "just because" and have never intentionally driven to places unfamiliar without benefit of a map or definite directions.

For one thing people say Hopkinton is a town...and they're not wrong.

Others say Hopkinton is a village...and essentially they are correct as well. It is a crossroads village.

Still others refer to it as Hopkinton City...and while it is not actually a city in the metropolitan sense, they are also right on target with their assessment.

Many call it "The Williamsburg of Rhode Island" because on a smaller scale it was, and still remains, a political, social, intellectual, and meeting place much like its counterpart in Virginia.

If you're coming from Westerly take High Street (Rt. 3) right through Ashaway, which, incidentally, is part of the Town of Hopkinton. Coming from Connecticut take Clarks Falls Road. When you reach the blinking light at the crossroads of Rt. 3 you've arrived.

As a town, Hopkinton is comprised of the quaint villages of Hope Valley, Ashaway, and Hopkinton City, with a total population of only about 6000 people. It's hardly a thriving metropolis, but that's why its residents choose to make their home here.

The actual village of Hopkinton is the administrative center of Hopkinton Township which was taken from Westerly and individually incorporated in 1757. It was named in honor of Governor Stephen Hopkins who presented the town with record books and a hand carved case in which to hold them. The village was originally called Hopkinton City...they were not two separate venues. The "old-timers" still refer to it that way, although most people have just shortened the name to "Hopkinton."

It was originally planned to have the government center to the south in the Tomaquag Valley, through which ran the highway between southern Connecticut and Newport; but later a turnpike connecting New London and Providence was cut through Hopkinton City in 1815. The subsequent introduction of railroad and steamboats further diverted travel to Hopkinton City.

A sensation occurred in Hopkinton City about 1796 when news circulated throughout the village that a gentleman and lady from the island would soon arrive on a visit in a chaise, a vehicle unknown here at the time. People, driven by their curiosity, flocked from far and near to see this

32

wonder when it arrived, climbing into it, drawing it around, and asking endless questions about it. It was not until 50 years later that Hopkinton City became a carriage and sleigh manufacturing center.

At one time local legend has it an old woman named Granny Mott lived in Hopkinton City, and who, it was firmly believed, was a witch.

The locals chattered that she could ride a smooth-shod horse over ice at full speed without incident. One day when she came to the home of Thomas Porter to ask for work, one of the Porter children thrust an awl up through the old woman's chair; and as if by magic, she did not move! After that no one doubted tales of her supernatural powers.

When the woman finally died, her daughter refused all help in preparing the body for the grave, which caused quite a stir among her neighbors. An explanation was ultimately given which still remains as Hopkinton legend to this day. It was reported that one of the villagers had been shooting hens the day before the old woman died; yet he had been unable to bring down one bird no matter how many times he shot at it. Believing it to be bewitched, he then substituted a silver button from his coat for a bullet. The bird then dropped, although the villagers were unable to find its body. That bird, explained the villagers in awe, was really Granny Mott, and her daughter did not allow them to see the body lest they know the truth.

Hopkinton is known for its well preserved 18th and 19th century homes, most of which are quite prominent on Rt. 3.

One of the more famous is the Deake-Utter House built in the early part of the 18th century, and the oldest house in Hopkinton City. It's a small one and a half story white frame house with a gable roof, dormer windows, stone chimney, and a one-story wing. History reports that the Deake brothers had jumped ship in Providence, fled into the woods in the southwestern part of the state, and settled in Hopkinton. In 1766 their property was sold to Abram Utter. Utter was one of the first cabinet-makers in town. His craftsmanship can be seen in many homes in Westerly and his work was largely fabricated in the old hat factory, for years one of Hopkinton's most important industries.

The Thurston House called the Thurston Mansion House in old deeds found at the town hall was built by Revolutionary War veteran General George Thurston about 1762. Later an addition was added and used as a store. After the General died, the store was carried on by his son Jeremiah who served as Lieutenant-Governor of Rhode Island from 1816-17. The house must have been lucky because a total of three Lieutenant Governors of the state lived in this historic home. There is a Thurston Cemetery south of the village on the west side of Route 3. It is also known as Hopkinton Cemetery No. 17.

RONA MANN

Opposite the Thurston House is the site of the Spicer Tavern. Joseph Spicer who toiled as a saddler, built a shop here about 1792. There were no horse-drawn wagons in Hopkinton at the time, and most of the work done by Spicer consisted of bridle and pillion making. As roads improved and horse-drawn vehicles became prevalent, harness making was added to his line of work. In 1806 Spicer purchased the tavern which became a popular gathering place and also served as a relay post on the New London to Providence Turnpike. History reports that at one time more than 60 horses were stabled here. The old tavern was later destroyed by fire in 1888, and its most famous proprietor, Joseph Spicer, along with his wife Mary, are buried near other family members in the little Spicer Cemetery on North Road, just northwest of the village, also referred to as Hopkinton Cemetery No. 15. There is a large monument erected there in the family's memory.

Another place of historic significance was the Second Hopkinton Seventh Day Baptist Church built at the southern edge of the village in 1835. The Union Meeting House built circa 1789 on a nearby site was enlarged and moved here in 1827. The town aided in this transfer and subsequent improvements with the condition that it could have the use of the building for Hopkinton Town meetings. This arrangement continued until 1860 when the present Hopkinton Town Hall was built across the street from the church. Since 1981 the original building has become the home of the Hopkinton Historical Association. The Seventh Day Baptists turned the property over in return for its maintenance and preservation; the landmark is now more than 210 years old. Today the First Seventh Day Baptist Church of Hopkinton has relocated to nearby Ashaway.

The crossroads of Clarks Falls Road, Rt. 3, and Woodville Road is a veritable lesson in history. In addition to the Thurston Mansion House, Spicer Tavern, and Deake-Utter home, the traveler encounters Williard Brown's Post Office & Shop. Brown served as Postmaster in Hopkinton City from 1873-1915 and also sold novelties and repaired watches there. The Thomas Wells House sports a sign circa 1785, the Thurston Wells House 1848, and the barn-red Benjamin Taylor House is circa 1789.

There have been many post offices in Hopkinton City over the years. In the 18th century it was often found in a store or tavern. At one time the post office operated out of the Spicer Tavern; later on it was in a general store. Today it's a modern affair just steps away from the town offices on Town House Road. At one time so many members of the town's Mills family filled the position of Postmaster that there was a Mills in the position concurrently for over 70 years!

Take a drive to Hopkinton City and begin to create your own journey. You'll find it's a journey to a city, but a city without malls, without restaurants, without movie theatres or hospitals or athletic complexes; but still a place with much to uncover. From the tiny cemeteries with mini histories engraved upon their headstones, to the historic homes wonderfully restored, to the many former post offices, there are legends and ghosts and whispers all about. Cock your head expectantly...you may just hear them!

34

The Road To: Laurel Glen, CT 06359

Know the expression, "If you blink, you'll miss it?" Chances are it was originally coined by someone who had taken a drive through the village of Laurel Glen, Connecticut in the Town of North Stonington.

North Stonington is comprised of the villages of Clarks Falls, Pendleton Hill, Ashwillet, Lantern Hill, the Village of North Stonington, and tiny, pastoral Laurel Glen.

Laurel Glen sits just north of Clarks Falls off Rt. 216 and Dennison Hill Road. Or you may reach the diminutive hamlet from Rt. 49 by going east on Puttker Road. At one time William Puttker was a prominent resident of Laurel Glen, a flourishing village with a post office and a center of manufacturing, but that is all part of its history now.

One of the more notable residents of the village was Deacon Solomon Barber born in 1823. A farmer's son, he grew up working on the farm while he attended school in the Ashbox school district. As he attained adulthood, his interest turned to the manufacture of cloth; and by age twenty-four he was actively working in the industry, eventually becoming proprietor of a large mill in Laurel Glen.

In 1894 the village residents decided Laurel Glen should have a church of its own, and a house of worship was erected known as the Fourth Baptist Church. The Glenites (a self imposed name for the hamlet's residents) wanted to associate the name of their church with the beauty of their area so the name was changed a short time later to The Laurel Glen Chapel.

But fortune was not to shine for very long on little Laurel Glen. Deacon Barber's factory burned to the ground about 1900. Not long after, Charles P. Eccleson of Ashaway, Rhode Island erected another building for the manufacture of shoe strings. Unfortunately this factory was also destroyed by fire leaving the economy of Laurel Glen in difficult straights.

To add to this misfortune, the post office was abandoned in 1911, just about the same time the one in Pendleton Hill closed. Simultaneously, the membership and activities of the church began to wane as well, and for awhile it appeared as though the Glen seemed to stop in time, as though it had ceased to exist.

This was compounded by the Hurricane of 1938 which took its toll on the tiny village by leaving a large hole in the church roof. This was the last straw, and the building was left to decay. In 1940, thanks to the efforts of George H. Stone, a storekeeper in the village of North Stonington and self styled local historian who contributed articles to the Westerly Sun in years past, the Laurel Glen Chapel was taken down and erected at the rear of the Third Baptist Church on Rocky Hollow Road in the Village of North Stonington. It is still there and still bears the name "Glen Chapel."

Driving through Laurel Glen on a brisk winter's day with the sun shining through the trees, it is difficult to imagine that once this was a thriving community with a post office, factory, church, school, and store. Back then there was also a boarding house owned by Frank Brown...a blacksmith shop, and a business that manufactured carriages and wagons.

With saltbox homes dating back to the 1700s, Lauren Glen also boasted a saw mill, a basket maker, and a charcoal industry.

Drive south from the West Laurel Glen four corners at Grindstone Hill and Puttker Road and you'll pass land owned at one time by farmer Israel Clark Chapman, by Jabish Breed Maine, by Dr. Wesley Hale, John Kynell, Charles Palmer, and nameless other Glenites who shaped a village by creating its history as well as its geography. While most of them and their families are long gone, they have left their indelible mark on the landscape; and if indeed you believe in ghosts, you can believe they still walk the rural roads and gaze across this hilly terrain.

Your "road less traveled" ends at the Clarks Falls Road where a bridge spans a babbling brook. Years ago those ghosts knew it as Pawkhungernock Brook, named for the hill than it ran past. These days Glenites know this brook as Captain Allen Brook, named for Captain Allen Wheeler who long ago joined the ghosts who will forever be remembered by the proud people of Laurel Glen. And now you too can know it as it is today...a bucolic little speck on a map dropped not coincidentally into your life as you continue on "The Road Less Traveled" in this little corner of the universe.

The Road To: North Stonington, CT 06359

It's a very peculiar thing really.

One minute you're on Rt. 2 heading toward Foxwoods Casino. And, of course there's traffic, but there's always traffic, regardless of the time of day. There's also a lot of lights, noise, businesses, activity. So you drive a little further until you see the turnoff and that small sign: "Village of North Stonington." And if you take that turnoff, suddenly, as though someone had turned off a light switch, you're in a different world.

Almost immediately you can see the difference. The restaurants and motels are replaced by large expanses of land...fields, farms, mini estates. And there are cows dotting the landscape, instead of gas stations and coffee emporiums. And it is so very, very quiet. Welcome to the Village of North Stonington where a tractor can motor down the road just as easily as that limo just back over your shoulder on Route 2.

North Stonington was settled in 1660. In 1720 the religious society formed to erect a meetinghouse for worship. Four years after that the village was officially named North Stonington, and it wasn't until 1807 that it was officially incorporated.

Agriculture was the chief business of North Stonington in the 1700s. Some 300 years later it is still a major source of livelihood for its 10,000 residents, only a handful of whom live in the village itself.

In the 1800s North Stonington was booming with tanneries, iron works, cabinet making shops, dye houses, and dry goods. It is no wonder then that the first name for the village was Milltown. This name stuck until the 1900s when the trolley began a run from Westerly to Norwich. The stop in the village was called "North Stonington," and the name stuck.

Upon entering the village, turn left on Main Street and get ready for a veritable history lesson! Nearly every building or private home sports a sign or nameplate on the front of the clapboards giving its original owner and/or the year the edifice was erected. Marcia Thompson circa 1804, Andrew Baldwin, Village Carpenter, 1819, Limperts Grist Mill, Wheeler Blacksmiths 1843...the list goes on.

Be sure and linger for a few minutes at the North Stonington Village Green. There's a sign beckoning you to stop, letting you know that the public is welcome here. There are benches so you can sit peacefully and enjoy the beautiful daffodils which have been carefully planted, listen to the fast-moving current of the stream as it rushes by, and take in a village where time has virtually stopped. Where there are no busy shops, restaurants, bars, or gas stations. Other than a paint store, antique shop, and a small gift shop, the streets are more about history than commerce. The latter may easily be found when you get back out to the bustle of Rt. 2.

A stop at the grange hall on Wyassup Road finds an Open House this day targeted for enticing young people to embrace the benefits of 4-H Club membership. Ben Murray is there helping out. Murray lives on Cossaduck Hill ...has all his life. "I'm born and raised here and wouldn't live anywhere else," he offers. When asked why that is, the immediate retort is "People and location. The people here are wonderful, simple, warm. And you can't beat the location. It's a beautiful village. A wonderful place to live."

Murray, who works with his father Jim in the welding and fabrication business, says that the addition of the casino just up the road has made a "noticeable difference, but still hasn't taken away from the charm of the village."

"We still like it here," he says, "It's like our own niche."

Another visitor to the 4-H Open House is Dan Holdridge, who grew up in North Stonington, although he lives in Mystic now.

"I'm a 9-11 survivor," says Holdridge. I worked for the Pentagon. After it got hit, I just came back here where life is simple and good."

Holdridge is right. Life in North Stonington is simple and good, albeit a study in contrasts.

Continue up Wyassup Road past the North Stonington Fairgrounds and just look at all that land! There's a lot of it in North Stonington. Homeowners have vast expanses of property. Some capitalize on it by gentleman farming; some just sell eggs and make a few extra bucks. Myrna Benedict tells of going to the upscale French restaurant, Le Cote Basque in New York City some years ago and telling the equally upscale, tuxedo-clad waiter that she was there because of "the egg money." She recounts her only reply was an arrogant sniff.

A left turn with a sign indicating Wyassup Lake beckons the traveler; and once there, a wonderful new treasure is discovered. A pristine body of water, a boat launch, and plenty of room to take a walk with a willing dog. And once again it is the very intense quiet that you cannot help but notice.

Leaving Wyassup Lake, go back up to the main road and turn down Ryder Road. Now you're driving parallel to the Shunock River, and in a short while, the rural road ends.

As quickly as you have encountered the Village of North Stonington, you are just as quickly deposited back onto Rt. 2. However a final glance in the rear view mirror reinforces the look back in history you have just witnessed; and somewhere in the distance you hear the first sound from the village you've heard all day: a plaintive moo.

The Road to: Old Mystic, CT 06372

It's really not a whole lot more than just a dot on the map that vaguely begins at the western end of the Pequot Trail; but oh, the stories, the history, and the reverberations contained within that dot!

Welcome to Old Mystic, not very far from the shopping village, the seaport, the factory outlets, and the bustle of tourism... but centuries away from all that in its geography and history.

First, the geography for you, good traveler, whether adventurous or armchair. To understand Old Mystic, you must first see how Mystic is configured. It is actually a valley with Lantern Hill at the top and Fisher's Island at the bottom. To the east are the Quocataug Hills, and on the west the Gallup Hill range.

Historians theorize that in prehistoric times the land was probably little more than an elevated plain. But a great ice sheet came down from the far north picking up enormous rock fragments in New Hampshire's White Mountains and Vermont's Green Mountains and plowed southward toward the ocean. On either side the plowed up ground was piled on top of the plain. When the land warmed and the ice melted, the glacier dropped a load of earth and rock in a pile which is now what we know as Fisher's Island, while the granite boulders were scattered throughout the rest of the valley. Years later the valley sunk, the sea came in, and the seacoast, as we now know it, was born.

The Pequot Indians had a small village on the river which originally they named "Sicanemous." Later pioneers named it "Mysticke" and settled there, eventually changing the name to "Mystic." When the twin towns of Mystic Bridge (originally called Pin Hook), and Mystic River (known as Portersville), 3 miles downstream grew larger and larger taking the Mystic name, the Post Office Department in 1890 changed the designation of the original area to "Old Mystic," and thus it has remained to this day. Geographically it borders the northeastern portion of the Mystic River from Exit 90 off I-95 to the intersection of Routes 184 and 201.

The railroad had not yet come to Old Mystic, but it was a stagecoach stop. Enterprising villagers quickly built two taverns to accommodate the new flow of traffic. Nightly, fiddlers played and travelers danced till it was time for "last call."

The original inhabitants of Old Mystic were English. Names like Brown, Chapman, Lanphear, Smith. Occupations were millworkers, blacksmiths, livery, ship builders, painters, millers, fisherman, storekeepers, ministers, fish mongers; and of course, even Old Mystic had the town drunk!

41

Saturday afternoons the locals poured into the streets for impromptu celebrations after their typical 12 hour workdays.

They drank and they partied, but they also were very religious in Old Mystic in the 19th and 20th centuries. At the time there were three churches in town, with standing-room only on many a Sunday.

The Civil War figures prominently in Old Mystic's history. Nearly every able bodied man in town was conscripted. Because of the war, one Elijah Morgan was the "county agent" at the time; and therefore the only person authorized by law to dispense intoxicating liquor. He owned the store across from the Methodist Church (a true dichotomy at the time since Methodists were violently opposed to drink), and had a barrel of high powered Bourbon well stored. Many in Old Mystic would hound Morgan for a drink, but he kept repeating this mantra: "When Vicksburg falls, we'll have a grand celebration." News of this announcement spread quickly, and news of the war now became the primary topic of the town. When finally Vicksburg fell and Lee's army was turned away at Gettysburg it meant two things to the local residents: the struggle was nearly over with victory certain for the Union forces...and it was time for Elijah Morgan to pay up! The entire community organized for a great celebration complete with a bonfire, decorations, food, and all-night imbibing!

Today, Old Mystic is still known far and wide for drink, but this time it's cider. The B.F. Cider Mill on the Stonington Road is a National Historic Landmark, having continuously made cider on that site since 1881. Clyde's is the only remaining steam-powered cider mill in the United States and a wonderful day's entertainment for the entire family. There are ongoing demonstrations, plenty of free parking, and cider to both sample and purchase. It is open 9AM-5PM beginning in August.

For the adventurous souls who love history and want to sleep where the oldest residents of Old Mystic once walked, the Old Mystic Inn built in 1784 beckons the traveler from its central Main Street location.

An octogenarian resident who only wanted to be known as "Richard" summed it up better than any writer could. "Old Mystic is about my people...my father, his father before him, and his father before him. It's about the Indian and the Fisherman, the Millworker and the man of God. The painter and the poet. And their good women and their strong children. It's about building up a place from nothing more than a heap of rock and making it something to be proud of. But don't tell too many people about Old Mystic. We want to keep it the way it is...the way it was... and hopefully the way it'll always be long after I'm dead and buried with the people who made this place."

The Road to: Pawcatuck, CT 06379

"What do you mean, less traveled,?" you say. "Why I drive through Pawcatuck almost every day!'

And that is just the point, Mr. or Ms. Traveler...you travel through it, but how many times do you stop, get off the beaten path, and really see what Pawcatuck is all about.

Pawcatuck is NOT part of Westerly, although we do tend to lump them together...i.e. Westerly- Pawcatuck Chamber of Commerce, Westerly Pawcatuck downtown activities, Westerly Pawcatuck this and that. Proximity does not make for duality, and Pawcatuck proves this with an individual history and profile all its own.

Pawcatuck is a village within the town of Stonington. Local history names Thomas Stanton as its first settler, joining William Chesebrough who actually founded the town of Stonington. The year was 1650, and Stanton was known throughout the new settlement as well as the region as The Indian Interpreter as he had erected a trading post in Pawcatuck to trade exclusively with the Indians.

If you travel to Lower Pawcatuck near the bend of the river you'll find a rock on which is inscribed: "Site of the house of Thomas Stanton, Indian Interpreter, 1651."

Stanton had come from England circa 1635, making a great study of the various Indian dialects. Because of his proficiency he was made Interpreter General of the New England Colonies, and additionally was one of the founders of the first church in Stonington.

Drive down Greenhaven Road to the Wequetequock Cemetery and you'll find Stanton's epitaph on the Town Founders' Monument. "A man of widespread and lasting importance to the colonies, and identified with nearly every transaction between the natives and colonists up to the year of his death." A wordy and heady epitaph indeed!

In 1669 Thomas Stanton was instrumental in planning the first highway known as the Post Road. The route was a mere four feet wide and ran from Old Mystic to the Pawcatuck Wading Place, just south of the bridge which today connects Rhode Island and Connecticut.

This same year the first shipyard was built on the Pawcatuck River. Shortly after this more shipyards sprang up, and today if you wind from downtown Westerly left onto Mechanic Street in Pawcatuck and follow the river around you will see evidence of their enduring presence. A little known bit of trivia tells us that Pawcatuck, and indeed the entire town of Stonington, is the only town in the state of Connecticut to actually border on the Atlantic Ocean. Other shoreline towns border Long Island Sound.

In Colonial times the Pawcatuck River was called "Great River" by the Indians who first inhabited the area. At one time it was also called "Narragansett River," and it was not until 1712 that the first substantial bridge was built over it.

Just north of this bridge was the S.P. Stillman carriage factory where stagecoaches were made. Today while there is no evidence of stagecoaches, the ancestors continue to live on in the small village.

Calvert Cottrell and Nathan Babcock founded the C. Cottrell and Sons Company on Mechanic Street in 1855. The company manufactured machinery, later specializing in printing presses which became famous all over the world.

In 1946 the Bostitch Company, famous for staplers and staples also moved to Pawcatuck's Mechanic Street from East Greenwich. At the time it was felt that it would be easier to find workers in Pawcatuck than East Greenwich.

Today Cottrell Manufacturing is gone, replaced by Cottrell Brewing, producers of a local beer; Yardney Technical Products has a large presence on Mechanic Street, but the Bostitch Company has pulled up stakes and moved back to East Greenwich. Still there are those who remember.

Gladys Porter, 89, a lifelong resident of Pawcatuck reminisces, "All the boys I knew either worked at Cottrell Manufacturing making that printing equipment or over to Bostitch. They didn't make a lot of money, but the work was steady, and if you hooked up with a guy who had one of those jobs you knew your future was secure."

Pawcatuck today is not so much a manufacturing hub as it is a study in contrasts. The older stately homes on Palmer and Moss streets and their adjoining neighborhoods stand proud, many of them over a century old, but well built to withstand the years of New England weather.

Across the road just off the Pequot Trail are the newer neighborhoods built on the well developed land off High Ridge Road. Here young families reside in homes just a few years old with central air conditioning and decks and swimming pools, yet built on land trod upon by the Indians, and built into a village by the colonists.

Travel up the Pequot Trail (Rt. 234) toward Mystic and the land becomes less suburban and more rural. Farms and farmhouses dot the roads along North and South Anguilla Roads and make for an interesting drive down this road less traveled.

Turn right on Anguilla Brook Road and drive just a short way to where the sign cautions you that this is the end of the town road and you are requested to proceed no further. Gaze down from the car window and you will actually see a tiny brook, its waters moving quickly under the road.

Once back on the Pequot Trail note the Open Door Baptist Church on your left. What a welcoming name for a church! The memories fairly dance with creative possibilities as you reflect back upon Pawcatuck's beginnings and wonder if indeed the weary traveller stopped for a rest and spiritual renewal at the thought of an open door.

Take a right onto North Anguilla Road. This is a beautiful ride! The road is well peppered with bends and curves, but stay the course and enjoy the view. From lush farmland to the Pawcatuck Little League field almost hidden between farms, to the saw mill to Adams Garden of Eden, site of the annual Garlic Fest, North Anguilla Road has a different complexion at each bend in the road. Turn right onto Elmridge Road, pass more farms, and within minutes you're at the popular Elmridge Golf Course, a few housing developments, and the junction of Rts. 2 and 49, signaling the beginning of a bustling pace of highways, casinos, and traffic.

Off the Post Road towards downtown history buffs will delight in the history and architecture of Pawcatuck's schools. Stonington High School was the first school built by the town of Stonington. Other town schools were built by school districts and eventually incorporated into the township. There had been a school on Palmer Street built in 1875, but it was destroyed by fire and never rebuilt.

And West Broad Street School, now 102 years old and still operational was considered in 1900 one of the most modern buildings of the time in this region. West Vine Street Elementary and Pawcatuck Middle School complete the village's educational picture.

At every junction, every STOP sign, every bend in the road, everywhere in Pawcatuck the old seems to meet the new. A building that may be over one hundred years old sits across from new construction. Where the actual downtown part of the village boasts homesteads from a colonial era, a short drive up the road will bring the presence of contemporary homes and businesses that support that growth.

From the markers of yesterday that remind us of Pawcatuck's long-ago roots, to the modern boatyards, industries, and residences of the present, Pawcatuck is a study in contrasts with a rich past filled with wonderful stories to delight future generations.

On Lathrop Avenue one recent Sunday morning local resident Ray Lopes was driving a small tractor down the street. When asked why he chose Pawcatuck for his home he replied, "I'm originally born in Mystic. I married a girl from Rhode Island, but I didn't want to live there. So I chose Pawcatuck."

And is he happy with his decision?

"Been here since 1957...you figure it out," he said. Then he smiled, revved up his motor, and headed down the hill. Toward home.

The Road To Perryville: 02879

There are historians who call Perryville a "ghost town," but an unnamed "local" pooh-poohed that and said, "Too small here, even for a ghost. And besides, nothing much to haunt."

While he may be correct about the size of the village, he is not correct that there's "nothing much to haunt." Like so many of the other treasures we have right in our own backyard, Perryville is worth a drive down the road less traveled.

First, some direction. Perryville is located just five miles east of Charlestown; yet there are folks who tell you they know they've heard of it, but aren't really sure where it's located. Not surprising. Other than an exit sign on Rt. 1 in either direction between Westerly and Wakefield, there isn't alot of hoopla surrounding the place. No neon, no advertising, no tourist draw. But that doesn't mean the place doesn't have alot to offer the purist who sees adventure down the simplest of country roads.

Perryville was named for Naval hero, Admiral Oliver Hazard Perry who was born here at Rocky Brook in 1785 to parents known locally as "Fighting Quakers." No slouch himself, Perry entered the Navy at the age of 13 and subsequently went on to distinguish himself during the War of 1812 as the hero of the battle of Lake Erie. After defeating the British squadron he uttered the now famous words, "We have met the enemy and they are ours." Perry was the first in history to defeat an entire British squadron and bring back every ship to his base as a prize of war. His flag with its historic message is treasured at Annapolis, and his blue sailor jacket, equally treasured, is part of the collection in the historic rooms in Providence; both just small memories of the man known for valor and quick action.

Perryville is not much more than a tiny part of the Post Road, (Rt. 1A), a bit of Ministerial Road (Rt. 110), and a stretch of Moonstone Beach Road, with only 4 or 5 additional smaller roads peppered with a few local homesteads.

One of the two area attractions is Carpenter's Grist Mill located on Moonstone Beach Road, built in 1703 with continuous operation for the last 300 years. It is a true working mill where Rhode Island Whitecap Flint Corn is stone ground by water power. In fact it is the only water powered mill currently operating in Rhode Island.

The water supply comes from Perry's Mill Pond just east of the mill. Ownership has changed a number of times over the past 300 years. Since 1986 the mill has been owned by Bob and Diane Smith of Wakefield who restored it in 1988. To their great pleasure in 1990 the mill was placed on the National Register of Historic Places.

Flint corn and Johnnycakes are native to Rhode Island and have been for over 350 years. When Roger Williams first arrived in 1636 he found local Indians growing flint corn which became one of the main food crops for both Indians and Colonists. The present strain has been developed as a result of work done with corn at the University of Rhode Island.

The coastal land of the South County area is perfect for producing the best whitecap flint corn, as both soil and climate conditions are ideal. Diane and Bob Smith open the mill every couple of weeks for grinding. "We encourage visitors to come then, says Diane. "Individuals, groups, school classes, scout troops...everyone's welcome. If they call us at (401) 783-5483 in advance, we'll let them know when we're grinding."

And grinding means Johnnycakes! At the recent open house marking the mill's 300th anniversary, more than 200 visitors were treated to Rhode Island's perfect little mixture of cornmeal and water, a throwback to the days when Indians made them for travelers and called them "journey cakes."

Just around the corner from Carpenter's Grist Mill is the Perryville Fish Hatchery. Begun in 1939 by a private company, the state took control of the hatchery in the 1950s which provides brown trout and rainbow trout to more than 50 ponds around Rhode Island.

The fish are hatched here from eggs and grown in the hatchery ponds till they're two years old. The hatchery's ponds are spring-fed by water that is kept at 50 degrees all year long and never freezes, so the trout can survive.

Unfortunately thousands of fish are lost each year due to predators who attack the hatchery's ponds, yet the Perryville Fish Hatchery is still able to grow enough fish to stock local lakes, ponds, and streams. In the spring just before the fishing season officially opens, hatchery workers load fish into special transport trucks and head off to stock local waters.

Visitors are encouraged to learn more by stopping at the Fish Hatchery Monday through Friday from 9AM-3PM. It is located at 2426 Post Road (RT. 1A) in Perryville.

"I like Perryville," enthuses Diane Smith. It's just a little hamlet. It doesn't have much, but it's quaint, it has good people, and a long history."

Funny...we think that adds up to a lot. On the road less traveled... this time to Perryville.

The Road To: Quonochontaug 02813

Quonochontaug...the name does NOT fairly roll off the tongue, but once there, it is a name and a place and a feeling that stays in your memory a long, long time.

Quonochontaug, or Quonnie, as it is affectionately called by the locals, is a part of Charlestown topographically, but truly it is its own place with its own identity and history and sense of pride. It is not at all like other parts of Charlestown.

The Niantic Indians named it Quonochontaug which, roughly translated, means "home of the blackfish." This subsidiary tribe of the Narragansetts came in the warm months of the year to fish. There is still some evidence of Native American life found in the area.

The best way to explore this special place is to drive north on Rt. 1 from Westerly, turning right onto West Beach Road. This long road takes you away from the noise and bustle of cars speeding along a modern highway in a hurry to get from here to there, and back into an era where things moved more slowly, land was prized, and people knew their neighbors.

As you drive down West Beach Road look for #262 on your left...the Asa Hoxsie Farmhouse. In the mid 1800s this was the Sherman Farm, and locals would go here for milk and eggs. Although there is now a private owner and it's no longer a farm, the home has retained its original appearance from the 1800s.

Everywhere you look there are rocks...rocks in the water, rocks along the breachway, rocky soil in all the yards. This is a throwback to the glacial periods some 21,000 years ago. With the melting of the glaciers, rocks, large boulders, and fine sediment called outwash were deposited along Quonnie's coastline. As the sea level rose, salt ponds and barrier beaches were formed. It is perhaps the large stones in the sea that best define Quonnie. The natives love it and have found beauty in it. Visitors stop and wonder about the how and why of it all.

Proceeding down West Beach Road from the Asa Hoxsie Farmhouse one sees new construction and remodeling going on amongst the older homes and cottages of the area. Some people resent this; others realize it is a part of the evolution and growth of the area. Everyone, however, agrees that Quonnie will never be a commercial area or tourist hub. If the visitor comes upon it, that's fine, but no tourist booth will be set out on the road, no tee shirts will be sold, no beach bars with loud rock and roll will beckon the throngs...not if the locals have a say, that is!

Shortly after the Farmhouse the visitor comes upon Quonochontaug Pond on the right side of the road. It is nearly impossible to miss with the large rocks jutting out of it. Pull to the side of the road, roll down your window, and just listen to the quiet. The rocks form beautiful shapes in the pond; and depending upon the time of day, light patterns form. It is an arresting sight on your trip.

Just down from this point on the same side of the road is the Pendleton Farmhouse built in 1910. It was Palmer Pendleton , a carpenter, who built several homes around Quonnie and helped with the construction of the Quonochontaug Inn. The home has had several owners since that time and has been extensively renovated.

You may wish to turn left on Kenyon Avenue and proceed directly to Central Beach, but a more rewarding itinerary awaits you if you stay on West Beach Road for awhile and give yourself up to the history that surrounds you.

If you choose to continue on West Beach Road you will encounter what's known as The Triangle where Old West Beach Road, Neptune Avenue, and West Street all appear to come together. It is also a faint border in the sand between what is known as Central Beach and what is West Beach. It is here that the oldest structure in Quonochontaug still stands...The Thomas Stanton-Nathaniel Sheffield Farmhouse, built circa 1700. The history of this structure is fascinating and long, involving a kidnapped Niantic princess and a rich family heritage. All of this and more may be found in the book, Quonnie...People, Places, and Pathways, compiled and written by Ann Schafer Doyle, the current President of the Quonochontaug Historical Society.

Doyle is the unofficial reigning Historian of Quonnie, succeeding the late Barbara Randall Mathews Adams who passed away in 1997. Since there had never been a formal written history of the area before this time, Anne Doyle literally sat at the feet of this woman who knew where all the bodies were buried, where the secrets could be unearthed, and where the old photographs might be found. Even as she lay dying in a hospital, Adams continued to impart her wealth of Quonnie information to Doyle, who then took on the project following Adams' death. She went to neighbors' homes, poured over photographs, listened to stories, and in the year 2000 the soft cover book was published. Every one of the 2000 copies sold out immediately, mostly to local residents. A second printing was completed last year with almost the same result.

The more you hear about Quonnie, the more you hear about the Hurricane of '38 and its impact on the area. There are two maps that accompany Quonnie...People, Places, and Pathways; the map prior to the '38 hurricane and the one after. As devastating as it was throughout the area, it was especially so in Quonnie where historic family homesteads, working farms, and scores of cottages along the Breachway were washed away. You reach this point easily by staying on West Beach Road. There used to be hotels here where fancy people with lots of money came from far away to stay for weeks at a time...to swim, to sun, to eat and drink, to dance. But the '38 Hurricane washed away all but the memories.

There were other "hang-outs" way back then at the Breachway in Quonnie. Three bowling alleys kept both the locals and summer people well entertained, while The Quonnie Casino was the place to socialize and have ice cream. Most notable of the locals during these years was Mother Brindley, proprietress of Mother Brindley's Store. Mother Brindley had come to Rhode Island from London to work in the Bradford dye-works. She opened her store on the Breachway in the 1920s selling candy, ice cream, and souvenirs to summer visitors. Just before the Hurricane the place became a tea room; then a place for the '38 Hurricane survivors.

Standing along the Breachway one afternoon one senses the sadness in the sand, intermingled with the stark beauty of the area on a winter's day. The wind blows strong here, the tall weeds move furiously in its wake. There is a light rain, the skies are overcast, the moisture shines off the big black rocks in the water, and yet for this one moment there is no more beautiful place on earth. This is why they came here, and this is why they stay...generation to generation. Farmer to farmer. Fisherman to fisherman.

Our road loops from the Breachway onto the coastline toward the east. Surfside Avenue leads you to East Beach Road. Take note of #468 which during World War II was a communications bunker linked by cable to both the Rt. 1 Lookout Station and the communication center on Block Island. Target practice was regularly held on East Beach, and people were not allowed to walk there.

East Beach Road eventually meets Rt. 1 and you're back in the present; but the best thing about Quonnie is that once you've been there, once you've talked with the locals or read Anne Doyle's book, you just can't get it out of your mind. So you turn around, this time starting your tour at East Beach Road and work backwards.

Bet you'll notice something new and different every time you go, because this isn't just any road less traveled. This is Quonnie.

The Road To: Rockville 02873

One of the urban myths about Rhode Island people is that they don't like to travel...that they pack a lunch to go from Woonsocket to Providence, or stay overnight when going from Westerly to Smithfield. While there may indeed be some truth to those statements, there is still an adventurous spirit in many people that needs frequent nurturing. If you are among them, this may be your story.

If your work keeps you primarily on superhighways, you might enjoy the opportunity of getting off at the next exit, of seeing where that side road goes, where the curve around the next bend takes you. In short, you might like to see the geography that shapes our neighborhoods.

If you find yourself in Hopkinton, leave I-95 at Exit 2 and turn onto Rt. 3 North. As you come down the steep hill into the village of Hope Valley you'll see a blinking light. Indeed this is the ONLY light in the village! Turn here and drive up Rt. 138 West, also known as Spring Street. As the road heads toward the Connecticut border and the town of Voluntown, you'll notice a small worn stenciled sign on the left: POST OFFICE. Turn here and find yourself on Winchek Pond Road. No pond in sight, take an immediate left onto Canonchet Road. Through the trees you'll see an old stone mill which houses the post office on the ground floor, and other businesses on the upper two floors. You'll have the sense that you have stepped back at least a half century, and nothing in that mill or the surrounding area challenges that feeling.

Upon leaving the stonemill parking lot, turn left again, and within a tenth of a mile you'll spot a well-worn arrow with a primitive sign for ROCKVILLE CEMETERY. Turn here, and you've turned straight into history.

It is a short, narrow, unmarked road that brings you inside the boundaries of the cemetery. Once inside is another sign: HOPKINTON HISTORIC CEMETERY #6. Obviously there are at least five more of them! But that's for another day.

This one is fascinating. It has charm, a lot of untold stories, and more than a sardonic touch of humor. The names on the stones are well-known ones...families who had founded and shaped this corner of Rhode Island: CASWELL, BARBER, WOODMANSEE, CRANDALL, KENYON, BABCOCK, BURDICK. Many of the grave stones are so old and weathered that even performing the school child's trick of putting a piece of plain paper on the stone and scratching over the indentations in pencil does not work. But then you see the dates: 1812, 1816, 1784. Perhaps most interesting is the grave of Benjamin Burdick, who "fell at Antietam 9/17/1862. Aged 23 years. I Die for My Country." Twenty-three years old! Had he been married? He lies in that plot alone, so it's doubtful. Had he sired children? Probably not. Did he ever have time on this earth to learn a trade, or build a home, or have a family? It seemed such a waste, but he died for his country, and

53

the family who put up that stone was proud to note that. Antietam! The name comes flying back from the pages of American history. It was one of the bloodiest battles of the Civil War, and here one can stand quietly at the grave of one of its veterans and give thanks.

Quite a ways in is the grave of Nathaniel Saunders who was born in 1869 and died in 1949. But Nathaniel is NOT alone for eternity. Not by a long shot! On his head stone after his name and dates of being is the following:

HIS WIFE
1873   Iva L. Johnson   1909

HIS WIFE
1876   Abbie E. Smith   1938

They're all in there together! Presumably, old Nate's in the middle and the ladies flank him like bookends. No doubt an interesting way to spend eternity.

Leaving Rockville Cemetery and making another left back onto the road you encounter a nature area just up the road. A sign indicates it is Long and Ell Ponds, and please would you help protect the plants and wildlife on this property. You would indeed. It is pristine, quiet, and a natural beauty.

From here on the road takes many twists and turns. It is largely woods with frequent small ponds. Places to walk a dog, or perhaps air out your soul for a bit. The quiet envelops. The simplicity of this road beckons; and yet you know there are secrets here. Secrets that long ago became personal history to the Kenyons and the Crandalls and the Burdicks. Some of it lives on. Some of it is gone, as it probably should be.

The road eventually becomes North Road in Hopkinton, peppered with homes, with cars and bikes in driveways, and people tending gardens, playing with kids, and living their lives. It ends at Rt. 3 where one can either turn north or south.

But before you do, look one more time in the rear view mirror, and see if just maybe you can catch another glimpse of the past before you make that turn and drive off into today.

The Road To: Shannock 02875

Shannock is like a man in an ill-fitting suit. Judged too often by what appears on the outside; yet when the well worn clothes are stripped away, there is a gem inside and in this case, a whole lot of history.

To begin with, Shannock doesn't know to whom it belongs. Part of the village is in Richmond , part is claimed by Charlestown. According to resident Keith Towne who has lived in Shannock for 28 of his 32 years, "Even the layout of Shannock is unique. Just going through town you cross the river twice as you go from Charlestown to Richmond and back into Charlestown."

Towne lives in the Columbia Heights section of Shannock, a miniscule neighborhood within a neighborhood on the edge of the village. Although many of the homes appear to need some paint or a new roof, there is a sense of neighborhood here not readily found in other areas. Towne attributes it to history.

"Shannock thrived in the 1700 and 1800s during the Industrial Revolution. It was a mill town. Columbia Heights itself was named after the Columbia Mill built by George Clark. Clark built the nearby housing so that his workers could easily walk between home and the mill. But when the mill closed, people left town and Columbia Heights was left as a low income area."

Those who enjoy the exploration of local history will find a rich one in Shannock. The village may be reached either off Rt. 112 in Charlestown by taking Old Shannock Road, or with access from Rt. 2 in Charlestown, turning at the Gulf station just north of Rippy's.

If you look for a place to have lunch in Shannock you won't find one. A Mexican restaurant used to be located right in the center of the village but left approximately three years ago when the bridge was re-done and the road was blocked for more than a year, severely hurting business. No access other than local foot traffic eventually forced the restaurant to another location.

Indeed there are few venues remaining in the tiny village. The Shannock Baptist Church, a fundamentalist church ,has been there 18 years, but with a strong presence. The church led by Pastor Dr. Scott Finkbeiner has extended that presence into today's highly technological world with the creation of its own website and time on public access television. On visiting the website one senses a tiny, yet tight-knit congregation, easily defining the very community scattered around it.

There is a small post office that serves just a couple of hundred people, and is so small that it closes for lunch every day. The postal clerk who works alone and lives in Ashaway cannot readily provide information. He knows little about Shannock, but directs us to the railroad tracks across the road. "The train doesn't stop here any more, but 30 or 40 years ago there was a station over there."

Keith Towne remembers it well, but for another reason. "Right there by the train station was a house. Mrs. Whiting lived upstairs, but downstairs she operated a penny candy store. She had to be about 90 years old, but she worked that penny candy store every day. We loved going in there."

But Mrs. Whiting is long gone, as is the store and the station. Now the tracks remain overgrown, and there is little local business, save for a sheet metal works.

What does remain is nature and a unique history. The Pawcatuck River divides the village between Charlestown and Richmond. There are two waterfalls, the most "famous" being Horseshoe Falls located along the road to Richmond. There's a monument there dedicated to the battle between the Narragansett and Pequot Indians over the possession of the falls. "That's where the cotton mill used to be," offers Towne. And Towne remembers the Shannock Spa, a small local store owned by Carl Richards located right next to the post office, serving as the local hangout for the village.

"But like everything else, when it closed, the people left."

Shannock at first blush seems to be a run down little piece of America that time forgot. Take a ride, examine it further, and find the beauty of the place in its rich history. Keith Towne summed it up best.

"Everybody that goes from Boston to New York by train passes through Shannock, but few look up and look out the window at what's really here. The neighborhood has changed. There are some new houses, and younger people with kids have moved here. It goes in cycles."

Just like history.

The Road To Usquepaugh: 02836

"Where is Usquepaugh?" you ask, wondering if we have made up a fictitious location for our road less traveled.

Those who live within the tiny confines of its boundaries smile knowingly, yet with a tinge of annoyance. They're used to this question. They hear it almost daily.

Usquepaugh (pronounce it "us-ka-paugh") is actually a small village within the town of Richmond, yet spilling over the border into South Kingstown. Its identity, if it even has one, is defined solely by its centerpiece: The Kenyon Grist Mill.

To reach Usquepaugh and the Mill your road begins in a highly trafficked area, yet transports you to the beauty and simplicity of yesteryear. From Westerly and Connecticut take Interstate 95 North to Rhode Island exit 3A. This puts you on Rt. 138 East surrounded by fast food restaurants and stores. Travel just 5 miles east and you will see the landscape begin to change.

From the strip plazas, past the ice cream stand, and then past the golf courses (and there are three of them in just such a short distance!), the road begins to wind back to a quieter, simpler time, sweeping you along to a place with a name seemingly larger than its land area.

You'll see the Kenyon Corn Meal sign on the right side of the road just before you turn onto Old Usquepaugh Road. The road is a narrow one with a few colonial style homes on both sides. When you reach the STOP sign, bear left onto Glen Rock Road. Immediately the Mill looms on the right hand side of the road.

This is the perhaps the last of the mills still operating in the area. Those that once activated the villages of Shannock, Kenyon, Hope Valley, and Hillsdale are now closed.

The Kenyon Corn Meal Co. is a small, family run operation whose grinding dates back to the 1600s. The large red mill you see on the right side of the road is a vintage 1886 structure. The original granite mill stones still slowly grind the grain to produce the texture and quality not found in the modern steel-ground flours of today.

When C.D. Kenyon bought the mill in 1909 he began producing corn meal in three-pound boxes. Back then farmers would bring their corn (known as grist) to the mill to be ground. Payment to the miller was a portion of the meal. Shipments were then brought to Providence by horse and buggy until 1916 when a Model T truck was purchased making deliveries easier. The mill has been owned since 1971 by Paul Drumm, Jr. and his son, Paul Drumm III.

They have kept the Kenyon Grist Mill a grist mill in the true Early American sense. It still operates much as an old time industry and is still in high production, producing its famous Johnnycake meal. Johnnycakes, for those who just came in on the train from Nebraska, were named from "journey cakes," because they were originally taken by sea captains on long voyages. They are made totally from flint corn which is then ground into a meal and then cooked into a small flapjack type cake.

The sign at the front of the building tells the visitor that "Tours are by appointment or by chance."

"It's really suggested that you call ahead," says Janell Hayes, a production sales assistant at the Mill.

There is a real sense of genuine pride here. A couple of other workers join Hayes in talking about the Mill and tell the visitor that in summer the owners are busy with fairs.

"They're at the Big E (Eastern States Exposition) in Springfield right now," says Hayes. "And they also did the Charlestown Seafood Festival, the Quonset Air Show, and the really big fair in Woodstock, Vermont."

The most popular product at fairs still remains Kenyon's clamcakes, with mixes being sold in local supermarkets, gift shops, by mail order catalogue, and at the Mill itself.

How big is Usquepaugh? The answers vary, but none is precise.

A worker at the Mill tells us "Just from here back to Rt. 138."

A Rhode Island atlas shows uneven borders with the village slipping away into Exeter, South Kingstown, and Hillsdale.

Just past the Mill up Glen Rock Road Charlie Cabeceiras tell us "It used to be alot smaller when I moved here in 1977. Now the houses have doubled."

Charlie and his wife Linda take advantage of the Mill's proximity and are small town entrepreneurs. A roughly drawn sign in the front yard and another on a tree beckon the traveler to stop for "Char-Lin Scorch," a homemade barbecue sauce with chili peppers.

The Char-Lin is named for its creators, but the "scorch?"

"Well," explains Charlie with a laugh, "We want people to know it's hot!"

Purchase a couple of bottles, although you wouldn't want to put it on your jonnycakes, and continue driving. Now you have a choice. Glen Rock Road winds up the road just a bit further, eventually intersecting James Trail and leading you into Exeter.

Or, if you are as taken by the name as we were, turn left just past Char-Lin's onto Punchbowl Trail. Almost immediately you'll be greeted by a sign on the left side of the road over a mailbox proclaiming, "Stewart Cohen lives here." A nice change from just a number or a last name. Obviously Cohen wants people to find him!

And why would anyone not want you to find this place? A little stream borders both sides of the road, well-wooded older homes mix with the new, and everywhere there are large trees that no doubt framed the village back when some of the first millers worked their stone grist mills made from famous Westerly granite.

Punchbowl Trail ends abruptly bearing left and becomes Smallpox Trail. This quickly leads you back to Rt. 138 and the 21st century; yet if you listen closely you may still hear the falls of the Queen's River that runs through the heart of the village. If you close your eyes you may yet see a miller working hard, "keeping his nose to the grindstone," and you will not soon forget the quaint beauty and long-ago simplicity of the road less traveled to Usquepaugh.

The Road To: Voluntown, CT 06384

As you approach Voluntown on Rt. 165 East there's a small sign at the side of the road which proclaims:
"DRIVE SAFELY - ENJOY OUR TOWN"

It's certainly not profound, but once you've explored Voluntown for a bit, you'll find this simple message is perfectly suited to the place.

No matter what direction you choose on your own personal road to Voluntown, Connecticut, very quickly you'll have the feeling that you've travelled far from home. But you won't be. Truth is, Voluntown is just twelve short, scenic miles from Westerly, but it has that far-away feel that makes exploration and discovery such a joy.

You can reach Voluntown from the east by taking Rt. 165 West from Rt. 3 in Exeter; 138/165 West in Connecticut will take you there, as will Rt. 216 through Clarks Falls from Rt. 3 in Ashaway, or perhaps the most scenic drive from the Westerly/Pawcatuck area is Rt. 2 West to Rt. 49. Rt. 49 is an amazing series of twists, turns, and bends in the road accented by farms, late Fall foliage, and home businesses selling everything from fresh eggs to real estate; from construction services, to an old weathered sign on a shingle advertising all at one location: "SQUASH...COOKIES...JAM... EGGS."

Rt. 49 intersects with Routes 138 and 165 right in the heart of bucolic Voluntown, and almost immediately you're beset with its story.

Voluntown has a rich history dating back to the 17th century when in 1696 Lt. Thomas Leffingwell of Norwich and Sgt. John Frink of Stonington petitioned the General Court to have a plantation granted to them suitable for settling a body of people. The only available land in the area was a six mile square parcel bordering Rhode Island. It was primitive, barren, and had been overrun by various tribes of Native Americans, although now no one lived there.

In 1701 a group of volunteers met in Stonington to make arrangements for survey and appropriation. It took four years until the boundaries were laid out: beginning at Ahvohsupsuck, a pond in the northern boundary of Stonington, they ran the line north one mile to a pond called Mahmansuck near the present western Voluntown boundary. Then a little east of north, 3 miles to a very small pond with a very large name of Toshconwongganuck, and then a mile and a half further to the site of the present Line Meeting House.

150 equal lots were laid out in the "Volunteer's land," but few were interested in settling there. The soil was poor, the location remote, and few inducements were offered to potential settlers.

King Phillip's War had raged with the Narragansett tribe stubbornly holding their ground. The future of the white men living in the area was dependent upon the outcome...would they return? Would they have a livelihood or something to which they could return?

As Americans have done throughout our history, men volunteered in large numbers. It was a long, hard, and bloody war. When it ended, the volunteers were tired and had no place to go. Therefore Connecticut gave these men large grants of land on which to raise their homesteads and start out again. These "volunteers" became the backbone on which Voluntown was founded as a monument to the men who freed the land.

A plaque at the junction of Rt. 49, 165, and 138 in the center of town tells the visitor that Samuel Dorrance, a Scotch Presbyterian from Glasgow came to this land with other Scotch Presbyterians. They were granted land separate from what became the Town of Sterling, and helped establish the first school in 1737. Dorrance became one of the first ministers in Voluntown, and the church grew steadily in its numbers.

Because of geographical proximity there was always conflict and unrest regarding those who lived "out of Voluntown." A meeting house was built, and those who lived over the Rhode Island line or on the borders of Plainfield and Killingly were granted equal privileges if they paid their proportion. This, however, was not always adhered to; therefore in 1734 it was voted that "all persons who live over the line in Rhode Island Colony shall be looked upon as strangers and transient persons."

After the turn of the century Voluntown finally reported progress.

There was one small cotton factory, two carding machines, two fulling mills, four grain mills, and two tanneries in full operation.

One of these mill owners, Ira Briggs, expanded his mill interest outside of town with purchases of stock in the Rockville Mills in Hopkinton and the Stillman Manufacturing Company in Westerly.

Traffic increased, and with it, another problem...wandering animals. Cattle and sheep were still interfering in highway traffic, so it was voted to restrain all cattle, sheep, and geese from running at large. Those owners who violated this ordinance were subject to having their livestock impounded at a fee of: 20 cents for cattle, 10 cents for sheep, and 5 cents for each goose.

Today's Voluntown is for the outdoorsman. Although its present population is approximately 2400, that number doubles in the summer largely because of the 26,000 acres of state forest, the Pachaug River, Beach Pond, and plenty of hiking, mountain biking, kayaking, and other outdoor sports.

Michael McCarthy, manager of Natures Campsites just off Rt. 49 in Voluntown moved here 8 years ago from Boston. Why did he leave such a thriving metropolitan area for such a small place?

"No traffic," he remarks succinctly.

McCarthy manages this seasonal business from May 1st thru October 15th and seems content to be idle the balance of the year.

"I watch the trees grow," he says sardonically.

When asked what he recommends people do in Voluntown, he growls, "Don't move here. People make for traffic. It's nice just as it is."

And he's right. A quick turn off Rt. 49 onto Shetucket Turnpike leads the traveller to Hartikkas Tree Farm with acres and acres of Christmas trees planted carefully in rows, growing, growing, growing for future generations.

Further down the road is Beach Pond, a wonderful recreation area which lies half in Connecticut and half in Rhode Island. Just ask any local...they'll tell you their territory is the best part!

If you're looking for a shopping mall, a movie theatre, a large supermarket, and a lot of activity, this is not your place. But if as David Nieminen of Nieminen's Gardens and Landscaping says, you're one of "the people who choose to live in or visit Voluntown because they have a great appreciation for the outdoors and for a natural place," then your next road less traveled must be to Voluntown, Connecticut.

The Road To Watch Hill: 02891

When you hear the name it immediately evokes a place for entertaining visitors, sightseeing along Bay Street, having a meal with a postcard-like view, waiting with great anticipation at the St. Claire Annex for a homemade ice cream treat, and capturing photographs of the lighthouse and the sprawling stately homes high on the hill. And of course there are the children screaming with unbridled joy as they experience their first ride on the Flying Horse Carousel.

But this is all about roads less traveled, so we're not going to point out what you may already know. Come along now that the season's ended for another year, now that the cold winds have begun to blow, now that the horses have stopped encircling the carousel and the Olympia Tea Room has shut down for the season...and see the real Watch Hill.

Watch Hill is best described as a Victorian village, a long time favorite hideaway for famous visitors and for the "beautiful people" who summered at Watch Hill long before they "found" Newport.

In the mid-1600s when the Greater Westerly area was being developed Watch Hill became important for its geographic vulnerability. With its wide open ocean frontage it was a likely target of pirates in the 1600s, and remained so throughout the Spanish, French, and Revolutionary Wars of the 1700s, the Spanish-American war of the 1890s, and straight through to World War I.

The area got its actual name during King George's War in the 1740s when a watchtower was built on the hill to warn against naval attacks, and was later used during the American Revolution. The original Watch Hill Light was built in 1806 and later replaced in 1856 with the current granite block tower.

It was the Industrial Revolution of the 19th century that forever changed the complexion of the area from that of a military presence to that of a much sought-after resort. It began innocently enough when the first lighthouse keeper, Jonathan Nash, rented rooms in his house in the 1800s. This lead to the first hotel ...The Watch Hill House which was established in 1833. The expansion of the rails brought the first tourists which created greater lodging demand. Thus quickly followed The Narragansett House, The Atlantic House, The Plimpton House, The Ocean House, The Larkin House, and the refurbished Watch Hill House.

This was rapidly embellished with the development of a bathing beach, bathhouses, hotels, and social and recreational activities; and therefore, a resort was born. Not only was Watch Hill becoming known nationwide as a vacation spot, but also as a seasonal residential community. Governor James Howard built the first summer residence cottage in 1870 followed by a group of Cincinnati industrialists who purchased a parcel of land in 1886 and subdivided it into 92 individual parcels. This led to the development of Wauwinnet, Everett, Niantic, Aquidneck, and Ninigret Avenues. Subsequent subdivisions of land followed and in 1889 the Watch Hill Improvement Society was formed, followed the next year by the Misquamicut Golf Club.

The summer "cottages" were hardly one room thatched roof configurations. They were homes to the national's most affluent and prominent citizens...governors, wealthy businessmen, socialites all comprising the growing summer population of Watch Hill.

The Great Depression brought problems to Watch Hill. Due to the economic crisis plus the aging of the community there were problems maintaining and managing the cottages and estates. Then came the hurricane of 1938 which virtually destroyed the ocean and bay frontages. Beaches, pavilions, and all of the homes on Napatree's Fort Road were carried away. But like the rest of the area ,Watch Hill slowly began to rebuild.

Many changes have occurred in Watch Hill during the last three hundred-plus years, but some things remain constant. No hurricane, no amount of storm-tossed seas, no economic depression could take away from the natural beauty of the area. Nature thrives here, and has carved her individual style upon the beaches, the configuration of the shoreline, and the wildlife. At Napatree Point a simple sign warns "Ospreys are nesting here. Please aid their survival. Keep your dog away from the nesting area."

There is a real charm to Watch Hill this time of year. One senses that the area needs this off-season to take a breath, to re-group, and to allow those who live here to appreciate the quiet. The parking lots are wide open; there are virtually just a handful of cars on Bay Street, most of them employees of the real estate companies which never seem to close.

At The Book and Tackle Shop racks of old books and magazines and postcards have been left outside, leaving the visitor to wonder if the owners are coming back to retrieve the merchandise, if it was left "for the taking," or if it's just there, pages blowing in the strong winds.

If you take this delightful sojourn, drive out the Westerly Road and make a right turn onto Foster Cove Road just beyond the Citgo station. Many people who live in the area for years have never seen any more of Watch Hill than its main roads, but it is along these narrow side roads that the real character of the place exists and its stories unfold.

Open your windows, crank up your heater, and listen to the sounds of Watch Hill in late Fall. You can hear the rhythm of the water, although the boats that once took up considerable space have been removed for the coming winter. Wild birds fly overhead, each with a distinct sound. Take the first left onto Popon Road and note the beautiful homes. Some have been named by the owners, such as "High Wicket," which makes one wonder if the owner named it for its meaning of a small gate or opening, or for its connection to the game of croquet, a sport of leisure favored by the privileged.

One road curves into another, always with a breathtaking view of a cove. Misquamicut Road leads to Potter Cove, Aquidneck Road to Foster Cove, and any road that leads you to Bay Street leads to Watch Hill Cove, where on this day a lone gull is bobbing in the water. The air is very still.

Turn up Larkin Road past the lighthouse and onto Bluff Avenue. The Watch Hill chapel is closed for the season, but one has the sense that its spiritual presence does not ever close. The Ocean House looms over the water on the right, standing proud and quiet, one season over and another to begin as it has for over 150 years. Turn on Ninigret Avenue and travel back to Westerly on Ocean View Highway, but make just one last foray as you bear left onto Yosemite Valley Road. This is a beautiful road with many curves and twists, taking you past historic old homes with sprawling landscapes, the well-manicured holes of the Misquamicut Country Club, and marshes, woods, and rays of sunlight hitting trees now devoid of autumn splendor.

The road deposits you on Shore Road and back to a busier pace. But if you listen hard, you might hear it. An echo. Watch Hill at this time of year is filled with echoes. Echoes of the past, echoes of a gull's plaintive cry, echoes of a lone automobile proceeding down Bay Street, echoes of children's laughter coming from the now bare carousel, and echoes of the men and women who shaped the rich history of the place we prize as Watch Hill on the road less traveled.

The Road To Weekapaug: 02891

The title may be misleading in itself. There is no real "road" to Weekapaug, although it is Noyes Neck Road off the Shore Road that will guide you there. An unnamed resident called Weekapaug "a curious speck on the coast in Westerly." And how right he was! It is little more than a beautiful seashell sitting nearly unnoticed in the sand. Its beach is barely a mile long. Its commerce is virtually non-existent. But once the visitor experiences Weekapaug they are drawn back again and again by the magnet of this simplicity, beauty, and uniqueness.

Weekapaug comes from the Niantic Indian dialect meaning "end of the pond," which is quite literal indeed as Weekapaug is at the end of a series of saltwater ponds. If you fly to Block Island you can look down and see a mile long barrier beach bordered by the Atlantic Ocean on one side and tiny ponds and marshes on the other. At the far end of these ponds sits Weekapaug, unassuming, yet very special to those who know it well.

The first homes were built in Weekapaug in the 1890s at a time when wealthy tourists were discovering the Rhode Island coast for their holidays. One of the first owners, Fred Buffum of Westerly, wanted to share this wonderful little place, so he began building an inn right on the beach. In 1899 the Weekapaug Inn opened with accommodations for just a handful of guests. Little more than six years later that number grew to more than 100 guests.

It was built out of a sense of New England conservatism, necessary and spare; and this hasn't changed in more than 100 years. If you want a big air conditioned suite with a coffee maker, color TV with all cable channels, double vanity, internet access, dataport, and more, there are hotels in cities that can give you those amenities. The Weekapaug Inn provides simply furnished rooms with no telephones or televisions in them, a small bathroom, and little else. Their amenities lie just outside the windows, doors, and decks. The beauty of the coastline, the crashing of the waves, the parade of seagulls...these are the accoutrements to this inn.

In September of 1938 Buffum's masterpiece on the beach was destroyed as the infamous Hurricane of '38 destroyed not only the Inn, but every house on the beach. It was little more than a miracle then that less than one year later the new Weekapaug Inn under the management of Buffum's son, Frederick, Jr. opened in the summer of 1939. This feat was accomplished by swift and purposeful action. Reconstruction began just days after the hurricane hit, with as many as 200 carpenters working on the property's restoration at one time!

Nothing else was built in Weekapaug after 1939 as all landowners deeded their beach properties to a common land trust so that no commercial nor private development could ever ruin the natural state of the area. And for the last 65 years, nothing has.

Since 1998 the Inn has been owned by the fourth generation of the Buffum family, Jim Buffum and his wife DeeDee. Although this is now Jim's full time job he readily offers, "But I worked there all the time when I was growing up."

Jim is proud that the Inn attracts families who check in wondering "What is there to do?" and check out knowing that having nothing to do except appreciating the natural state of the land and the people around them may indeed be the very best thing to do.

"We send out a letter to our guests before they arrive, so they have some idea of what to expect," says Buffum. "The interesting thing is it's the kids who push the parents to come back year after year. I think families are so busy today with both Mom and Dad working two jobs and no one having time for each other, that we afford them a way for kids to actually see their parents and spend time with them without a lot of outside distraction."

Weekapaug, tiny as it is, still boasts two separate beaches, the mile long beach by the Inn and the Fenway which is found about a half mile away. The Inn's beach is designed for guests with a bathhouse, changing rooms, and beach umbrellas on site. The Fenway caters more to children with easier access to the water, a jetty to explore, and lots of interesting rocks.

Residents fiercely protect the unprotected, unspoiled nature of this little piece of Westerly. The Weekapaug Foundation for Conservation is a non-profit organization boasting some 750 members who have amassed over 105 acres in Weekapaug. Their mission is simple: identify, protect, and maintain. They identify suitable open space for conservation, following up with appraisals, title searches, and engineering studies. Then this land is protected through outright purchase. Lastly, it is consistently maintained by the clearing of rocks and brush, frequent mowing, planting, mending, regular maintenance, and ongoing preservation of plant and animal species, specifically those that are endangered.

Most residents of Weekapaug live there year round. They quietly keep up the maintenance of their own homes and land and the preservation of the area they fiercely protect from growth or urbanization.

Jim Buffum sums it up with thoughtful reflection. "Weekapaug is very much a step back in time to an old fashioned summer, but it's also very much a part of the Westerly community. And I'm so proud that Westerly continues to grow and better itself all the time."

Just another stop along a road less traveled...this time the road to Weekapaug... the "end of the pond."

RONA MANN

The Road To White Rock: 02891

Joe Hebert was working in his yard on a recent afternoon when he was asked about White Rock.

"Go inside and see my wife, said Hebert as he addressed the request. "I'm originally from Hartford. Only been here 52 years, but she was born here. She can tell you all about White Rock."

Mary Hebert is a friendly, delightful woman who voluntarily turned up her hearing aid so she could be right on target, but when asked, "What is it that's special about White Rock?" she deferred by saying, "Go to the mill. It's just down the road. Everything about White Rock starts and ends with the Mill."

The Mill Mary spoke of is Griswold Textile Print, Inc. To reach the Mill and thus the heart of White Rock, drive down Canal Street from downtown Westerly. All the way down. And when you think you're done, drive some more.   Just past the bridge that leads to Rt. 2 in Connecticut (the locals call it "the bridge that was closed for several years") is White Rock Road, a 45 degree angle left turn. Turn here and step back into an old mill village that is still, quietly an integral part of the fabric of Westerly, Rhode Island.

In 1876 at an Independence Day gathering also marking the country's Centennial Celebration, a banner flew over the village with the inscription:

"White Rock...Small but Firm"

It was a portent of history to come, for some 128 years later the tiny village with few businesses and just a handful of residents still remains small, but firm.

The most imposing presence is indeed the Mill. You'll find it after you've driven past the Gingerella Sports Complex and the road that leads to Springbrook Elementary School. First built in 1849 and enlarged in 1877 the mill exists today as a successful operation, even though the Hurricane of '38 wiped out the dam and ripped off the roof of the building. The original turbines that powered the sewing machines in those days are still housed in the basement.

Vice President and owner Paul Bergendahl whose family has owned Griswold Textile for many decades explains that although the mill has a worldwide reputation as a high end printer of decorative fabrics for upholstery and draperies, its local profile is deliberately kept low.

"We don't advertise. A lot of people don't even know we exist," offers Bergendahl, "But we employ 28 people full time. Years ago nearly this whole village was comprised of mill employees."

The original owners of the mill built twelve double houses in a line across the street for managers and employees. Many of these homes still stand today. Right in the center of White Rock is Cottage Street with smaller houses that served as lower income housing for mill employees.

Even though Bergendahl does not advertise nationally or locally, there is a small store at the mill, open to the general public Monday through Friday 8AM-2:30PM. It is here that bargain hunters can find factory seconds and overruns of high quality fabric for not a lot of money, but potential customers, take notice. Signs through the store caution the consumer, "New Policy...Cash NOT accepted. Credit cards only."

Bergendahl is the sole salesman for the company, having a longstanding relationship with large decorative houses worldwide. He points with pride to the fact that the mill still prints their fabric on 50 yard long tables.

Town records indicate that White Rock began in April of 1675 when a 700 acre parcel of land was sold to Major Brain Pendleton from John Payne. It is bounded on the west by the Pawcatuck River which runs to a large white oak tree. The tree stands by a great rock located in the vicinity of the mill. From town records it appears that the name "White Rock" evolved from this simple matter of geography.

While the mill in its heyday employed some 150 people the work ethic of the day was a good deal different from today. Working twelve hours a day, six days a week, the employees produced some 2700 yards of fabric in a 78 hour week.

In 1871 B.B. Knight and his brother Robert bought the mill for the production of their famous "Fruit of the Loom" cotton sheeting. The Knight brothers were so successful that they doubled the size of both the mill and the village by 1877. Following World War I, the Knights sold their interest in the Mill and the property was sold at public auction in 1927. Additionally at this time 34 village homes were sold as well, although the mill itself did not go up for auction. It stood idle until 1931 when the

Narragansett Finishing Company moved into the property, however the owners fell on hard times; and in 1945 it went into receivership.

In 1945 Frank Ahern, a Norwich businessman, bought the property, did extensive repair and renovation, and in 1948 the Griswold Textile Company moved from Norwich to White Rock.

There isn't a whole lot else in the tiny village, save the large white structure on top of the hill that hums with the very pulse of the place: the White Rock Inn.

According to employee, Carol Burge, the inn was built circa 1845 to house the workers while the mill was being built. Originally called "The Village Inn," the White Rock Inn has a large parking lot; and for a good reason...it is always full.

Burge explains it simply. "It doesn't look like much, but it's a great place. I don't think you'll find a cheaper beer in the area, we have great food, and all day Friday we feature a steak dinner special till we run out. And we always run out."

The structure is large and sprawling. Inside there is hardly a seat available, and each time the door opens bringing new patrons, the crowd turns around seemingly in one motion to see who it is, and to greet the familiar face, or perhaps just smile at a stranger.

"It's a friendly place, explains Burge. "People from out of town coming over the White Rock Bridge often make a mistake when looking for downtown Westerly and turn left. They don't realize it's a dead end street. So when they get to the end of the road and see the White Rock Inn quite often they'll come in for a drink or some food, and when they do, whether they're from Massachusetts or Connecticut or wherever, they always find their way back."

White Rock...just a speck on the map, a little village within a small town nestled in small town America, but a very colorful stop on the road less traveled. As Carol Burge describes the White Rock Inn, so the entire village may be described, "It's a funny little place...but the regulars keep it going."

The Road to: Wood River Junction
02894

It's really all about the railroad, although the name might conjure up a T.V. sitcom or perhaps a tiny southern town with a local bar in the center of the village and a proprietor aptly named "Pops."

Fact is, the Wood River Junction we know is nothing like this. There isn't a bar for miles, it isn't fodder for a T.V. sitcom, and as far as anyone in the area knows, no one is, or has been called, "Pops."

"The thing about Wood River Junction," said a local who wanted his anonymity, " Is that once you found it, you're probably just about out of it."

He's right. Wood River Junction is in the southwest corner of what's known as the 1709 Shannock Purchase. It is located at the very southern boundary of the town of Richmond, bordered on the south by the Pawcatuck River, on the west by the Village of Alton, and on the east by Meadow Brook.

Prior to 1873 the small plot of land was known as Richmond Switch because it was where trains such as the Hartford Railroad, the New York, the Providence-Stonington, and the New Haven met together for passengers and products to "switch" to their destinations.

In 1873 when the Wood River Branch line was established the name of the village was changed to Wood River Junction because the train played such an important part in transporting people "all the way" from Richmond Switch to Hope Valley.

Others in town feel that it was the old Wood River mills that precipitated the name change, while still others attribute it to the fact that most of the wood supplied to the railroad came from Wood River. This friendly difference of opinion has never been resolved to this day.

Still, the centerpiece of Wood River Junction was the rail line which provided the incentive that lead to the development of homes, business, and land. An article from a very old and unnamed area newspaper asked:

"If two men started out for a trip around the world, and one starts from Hope Valley and the other from Wood River Junction, can the Hope Valley man reach Wood River Junction (by the usual route, of course) in the time the other completes the circuit of the Globe and reaches his starting point at the Junction?"

71

To reach the outlying areas of Richmond, especially the very "distant" Hope Valley, the Wood River Branch train was born. Locals often joked and called it the Tooneyville Trolley, yet it operated for 74 years between Wood River Junction on the New Haven Shoreline and Hope Valley. This line served 15 manufacturing establishments of the era, survived two World Wars, several depressions, a handful of train wrecks, and a disastrous flood in 1927 which wiped out the Woodville Covered Bridge and several sections of the track.

It was a group of local merchants led by Roy Rawlings a Hope Valley grain and feed miller who succeeded in getting the New Haven to take over the operation. In 1937 the New Haven sold the line to Rawlings for $301. His daughter, Lucy Rawlings Tootell became Vice-President at the time, the only female railroad Vice-President in the United States.

Mrs. Tootell now 91 and living in North Kingstown still marvels at the turn of events when she tells the story:

"My father, Roy Rawlings, was originally from Illinois. He met my mother who was born in Providence when both of them were living and working in New York City as actors in the very early 1900s. Together they toured the USA in a play about Abraham Lincoln's life. When they settled down and married it was in Richmond where my father bought 1000 acres of land. Father had a mill in Hope Valley where he made grain for farm animals. When the railroad was beginning to lose money and about to be closed down they came to my father and offered him ownership. He told them 'I have no money, not the kind of money it takes to own a railroad.'

"But they kept asking him how much he did have. He finally laughed and told them that he had $301. and they said, 'Sold!' And that's how my father came to own a short line that ran only 5.6 miles between Hope Valley and Wood River Junction."

Although, according to Tootell, she only had a "classic education" and no bookkeeping or business experience, she was sent as the new Vice President of the Wood River Branch Line to a meeting in New York of the American Short Line Railroad Association. Tootell recalls this being in the early 1940s when she was just 32 years old. As the only woman in a room of 1000 men she most certainly was "noticed" and asked to stand when introduced to the large crowd as the only female Vice-President in the country.

"I'm glad they didn't ask me to speak to that many people, but I sure enjoyed the applause of 1000 men!"

The early names of the Wood River Junction families are familiar names all over our area even today: Terranova, Hoxie, Crandall, Kenyon, Collins, Burdick. One of the most important figures of the era was George N. Ennis, who was born in Charlestown and moved to Richmond to open a general store in 1843. Today that general store no longer exists...there really are no retail stores of any kind in Wood River Junction.

Maureen Black, the Officer-in-Charge of the tiny Wood River Junction post office says that other than the Charbert Mill in Alton, a small woodworking shop, and the Chariho School Department on Switch Road there really are no business deliveries.

And how many people reside in Wood River Junction?

"The exact number is hard to tell," says, Black. "The one rural route carrier we have has 250 deliveries. And we have just over 100 boxes rented."

The post office which sits right at the junction of the Alton Bradford Road and Switch Road is just 535 square feet according to Black and was built in January 1965. Like many rural post offices hours are limited. "We close for lunch every day from 1-2 PM."

Does Maureen Black enjoy such a tiny domain? "I love it. I love talking with everyone. I love the small hometown feeling you get here. I can give the local people good service, and in many cases I know what they want before they ask."

Wood River Junction has also enjoyed a statewide reputation for being the coldest spot in Rhode Island. In January and February of 1961 local residents recorded 16 straight days of temperatures below zero, one day bottoming out at a bone-chilling - 27 degrees! It is believed that this phenomena occurs because Wood River Junction is in a valley just a few feet above sea level. When cold air flows from Hope Valley to Wood River Junction it meets cold air flowing from Shumunkanug Hill (in Alton) to the Junction, thus forming a frost hollow. Thus temperatures in the tiny hamlet are almost always 15 degrees colder than those in Providence.

Wood River Junction is most definitely a "road less traveled." Many area residents have never heard of it; and those who have are not exactly sure where it begins or ends.

But just ask anyone who lives there now, or who lived there long ago. The story of this "road" will always begin and end with the railroad.

Epilogue

There are now more pages turned on the left side of your lap than on your right.

So you think you've read the whole book, right? Wrong. There is no "end" to a book about "roads less traveled," because to each person who takes them, and for each new journey or adventure, there is always something new. History isn't past tense. It evolves. It rewrites itself. It continues long after the pages of a book disintegrate, and certainly long after we are here.

Shakespeare wrote, "What is past is prologue." How very accurate that statement was and continues to be along roads less traveled and ghosts not yet met.

I've written the first 26 chapters. The next one is up to you.

...Rona Mann

RONA MANN

RONA MANN

RONA MANN

RONA MANN

About the Author

Rona Mann started writing in her native New Jersey at the age of 8. By the time she was in high school she had a weekly column in the local newspaper and went on to contribute articles to national magazines. She holds a B.S. degree in theatre and an M.S. degree in communications from Syracuse University and has performed both in summer stock and off Broadway productions. Mann lives in Rhode Island where she teaches advertising and public speaking adult education courses, is active in the Westerly Rotary Club, performs a one-woman nostalgia show throughout the country, and lives happily with her husband, Dave and their two cats. "Ghosts Along the Road" is her first book.

Printed in the United States
30194LVS00006B/397-417